THESE DEMONS

by Rachel Bellman

‖SAMUEL FRENCH‖

FOR AMATEUR PRODUCTION ENQUIRIES

UNITED KINGDOM AND WORLD
EXCLUDING NORTH AMERICA
licensing@concordtheatricals.co.uk
020-7054-7298

Each title is subject to availability from Concord Theatricals, depending upon country of performance.

---

written permission of the publisher. No one shall share this title, or part of this title, to any social media or file hosting websites.

The moral right of Rachel Bellman to be identified as author of this work has been asserted in accordance with Section 77 of the Copyright, Designs and Patents Act 1988.

USE OF COPYRIGHTED MUSIC

A licence issued by Concord Theatricals to perform this play does not include permission to use the incidental music specified in this publication. In the United Kingdom: Where the place of performance is already licensed by the PERFORMING RIGHT SOCIETY (PRS) a return of the music used must be made to them. If the place of performance is not so licensed then application should be made to PRS for Music (www.prsformusic.com). A separate and additional licence from PHONOGRAPHIC PERFORMANCE LTD (www.ppluk.com) may be needed whenever commercial recordings are used. Outside the United Kingdom: Please contact the appropriate music licensing authority in your territory for the rights to any incidental music.

USE OF COPYRIGHTED THIRD-PARTY MATERIALS

Licensees are solely responsible for obtaining formal written permission from copyright owners to use copyrighted third-party materials (e.g., artworks, logos) in the performance of this play and are strongly cautioned to do so. If no such permission is obtained by the licensee, then the licensee must use only original materials that the licensee owns and controls. Licensees are solely responsible and liable for clearances of all third-party copyrighted materials, and shall indemnify the copyright owners of the play(s) and their licensing agent, Concord Theatricals Ltd., against any costs, expenses, losses and liabilities arising from the use of such copyrighted third-party materials by licensees.

IMPORTANT BILLING AND CREDIT REQUIREMENTS

If you have obtained performance rights to this title, please refer to your licensing agreement for important billing and credit requirements.

NOTE

This script may have changed during rehearsals and may differ from the final production.

THESE DEMONS was first produced by Tanya Truman Productions and Theatre503, and received its world premiere at Theatre503 in London on 26 September 2023. The cast, creative team and production team were as follows:

LEAH . . . . Olivia Marcus
DANIELLE . . . . Liv Andrusier
MIRAH . . . . Ann Marcuson

Playwright . . . . Rachel Bellman
Director . . . . Jasmine Teo
Creative Producer . . . . Tanya Truman
Set & Costume Designer . . . . Sophie Firth
Lighting Designer . . . . Skylar Turnbull Hurd
Sound Designer . . . . Niamh Gaffney
Movement Director . . . . Laura Wohlwend
Costume Associate . . . . Peiyao Wang
Production Manager . . . . Laurel Marks
Stage Manager . . . . Waverley Moran
Assistant Director & Cover . . . . Lauren Koster
Associate Producer . . . . Bethany Cooper

TANYA TRUMAN PRODUCTIONS is a London based production company focusing on developing and amplifying new, female led contemporary Jewish writing.

Theatre503 is at the forefront of identifying and nurturing new voices at the very start of their careers and launching them into the industry. They stage more early career playwrights than any other theatre in the world – with over 120 writers premiered each year from festivals of short pieces to full length productions, resulting in employment for over 1,000 freelance artists through their year-round programme.

Theatre503 provides a diverse pipeline of talent resulting in modern classics like *The Mountaintop* by Katori Hall and *Rotterdam* by Jon Brittain – both Olivier Award winners – to future classics like Yasmin Joseph's *J'Ouvert*, winner of the 2020 James Tait Black Prize and transferred to the West End/BBC Arts and *Wolfie* by Ross Willis, winner of the 2020 Writers Guild Award for Best New Play. Writers who began their creative life at Theatre503 are now writing for the likes of *The Crown*, *Succession*, *Doctor Who*, *Killing Eve* and *Normal People* and every single major subsidised theatre in the country now boasts a new play by a writer who started at **Theatre503**.

THEATRE503 TEAM

Artistic Director . . . . Lisa Spirling
Interim Executive Director . . . . Jules Oakshett
Literary Manager . . . . Steve Harper
Producer . . . . Ceri Lothian
General Manager . . . . Emily Dickson
Carne Associate Director . . . . Jade Lewis
Literary Associate . . . . Lauretta Barrow
Trainee Assistant Producer . . . . Tsipora St. Clair Knights
Technical Manager . . . . Misha Mah
Marketing Officer . . . . Millie Whittam
Administrator . . . . Lizzie Akita
Development Coordinator . . . . Heloise Gillingham

Theatre503's work would not be possible without the support of the following individuals, trusts and organisations:

We are particularly grateful to Philip and Christine Carne and the long-term support of The Carne Trust for our International Playwriting Award, the 503 Five and Carne Associate.

503Patrons: Ayla & Jon Hill, Berlin Associates, Caroline & Tim Langton, Cas & Philip Donald, Catharine Roos, Céline Gagnon, David Baxter & Carol Rahn, DavidsonMorris Solicitors, Eilene Davidson, Eric Bensaude, Erica Whyman, Freddie Hutchins & Oliver Rawlins, Gaskell & Jennifer Jacobs, Geraldine Sharpe-Newton, Ian Mill KC, Jack Tilbury/ Plann, Laura Riddeck, Lisa Swinney, Lou Wilks & Tom Gowans, Louise Rawlins, Marcus Markou, Marianne Badrichani, Matthew Marren, Nick Hern Books, Pam Alexander & Roger Booker, Robert O'Dowd, Sally O'Neill, Sean Winnett, Steve Winter, The Bell Family, The Bloor Family, United Agents and all our 503Friends and Share the Drama supporters.

503 Slate Philanthropic Co-Producers: Cas & Philip Donald, Concord Music Group, Inc, Eilene Davidson, Gordon Bloor, Hania Farrell, Jean Doumanian/Peony NY LLC, Kater Gordon Productions Ltd, Kofi Owusu Bempah, Lucas Achkar, Marcus Markou, Ocourant Ltd, Royce Bell, Lucas Achkar, Trish Wadley Productions.

Arts Council England Grants for the Arts, Backstage Trust, Battersea Power Station Foundation (Right to Write), Cockayne Grants for the Arts (503 Productions), Concord Theatricals (503 Playwriting Award), Garrick Charitable Trust, Noel Coward Foundation (Rapid Write Response), Theatres Trust, The Foyle Foundation, The Orseis Trust (503Five), Wandsworth Borough Council, and Wimbledon Foundation (Five-O-Fresh).

Our ongoing thanks and gratitude to Three Cheers Pub Co. for our home above The Latchmere Pub.

CAST

OLIVIA MARCUS | LEAH

Olivia plays Megan (Magnet Girl) in Disney Plus's *Extraordinary* and has upcoming roles in *Starstruck* and *Bad Education*.

Further TV credits include: *Stath Lets Flats* and BBC3 pilot *Amicable*.

She played Jane Seymour and Katherine Howard in the stage adaptation of Hilary Mantel's *The Mirror and the Light* (RSC/Gielgud Theatre) directed by Jeremy Herrin.

Further theatre credits include: *Lord of the Flies* (Theatr Clwyd/Sherman Theatre) and *Everything Must Go* (These Girls Theatre).

Olivia also stars as the title role of Yentl in BBC Radio 4's *Yentl the Yeshiva Boy*. She trained at Royal Welsh College of Music and Drama.

LIV ANDRUSIER | DANIELLE

Liv is an actor, singer and writer from London. She graduated from RAM in 2021.

Liv is a 2023 Stage Debut Award nominee and Offie Award winner for her leading performance in *Ride*. The production played at Leicester Curve and Southwark Playhouse's Elephant Theatre following a critically acclaimed run at Charing Cross Theatre.

Further theatre includes first cover Jo March & u/s March sisters in *Little Women* (Park Theatre).

She began her career in *Chitty Chitty Bang Bang* at the London Palladium, followed by Annie in *Annie* at the Bloomsbury Theatre, and then as the youngest of the Lovely Ladies in Tom Hooper's *Les Miserables* (Working Title).

On screen, her role in *Pennywort* (BFI) saw her nominated for Best Supporting Actress at the Midlands Film Festival by a panel that included director Shane Meadows. She won Sky's 'Play In A Day' competition and performed alongside leading industry figures on Sky Arts during the pandemic.

Training: Royal Academy of Music.

ANN MARCUSON | MIRAH

Trained at Webber Douglas.

Theatre includes: *The Curious Case of Benjamin Button* (Southwark Playhouse), *Brendan, Son of Dublin* (ICC), *Two Ladies* (Bridge Theatre), *Checkpoint Chana* (Finborough), *The Mighty Walzer* (Royal Exchange Theatre), *Curious Incident of the Dog in the Night-Time* (National Theatre, NTP and Gielgud), *The Lottery* (Bury Court Opera), *The Glass Slipper and Bloodhound* (Northern Stage), *The Family Reunion* (Donmar Warehouse), *Little Wolf and Hard Love* (Hampstead Theatre), *Needle* (Soho Theatre), *Sweet Dreams* (Sphinx Theatre Company), *Strange Love* (Young Vic), *Brassed Off* (York Theatre Royal), *I Dreamt I Dwelt in Marble Halls* (Tricycle/Watermill, Newbury; Times Best Performance), *Pinocchio* (Regent's Park Open Air), *Twelfth Night* (Keswick), *Little Shop of Horrors* (Basingstoke Haymarket), *Diary of Anne Frank* (Harrogate Theatre), *Over Ruled* (King's Head).

Film and TV: *The Power* (Sister Pictures/Amazon Studios), *This Is Going To Hurt* (BBC), *Redemption Day* (H Films), *Emmerdale* (ITV), *Bancroft* (ITV Studios), *The Divorce* (UK Jewish Film Festival), *A Place For Everything* (BFI), *Shark* (Met Film), *Relentless* (October Films), *Family Affairs* (Freemantle), *The Bookworm* (BBC).

Radio: *Sabbat*, London Radio; *The Middle Eastern Cookbook*, Radio 4.

CREATIVE

RACHEL BELLMAN | PLAYWRIGHT

Rachel is a London-based writer and lyricist. Perpetually drawn to narratives that are unique, meaningful and strange, her current projects include the musical *Game Theory* developed by Perfect Pitch and produced in concert at The Lowry in 2021; *90 Seconds to Midnight*, a collaboratively written and devised project with Timelapse Theatre; and *How to Escape* developed with young people at Liverpool Empire. In 2019 she won the New Music Theatre Award for *The Dickens Girls*, which was subsequently commissioned and produced as part of BYMT's summer season at the New Wolsey Theatre.

Other past projects include *So-Called Gen Z* produced by PQA at the 2019 Edinburgh Fringe, commissions from JW3 and Perfect Pitch, and various short plays produced in London. She has been a three-time finalist for the Stiles + Drewe Best New Song Prize, and has taken part in the BOOK Music & Lyrics advanced composer/lyricist workshop, MMD writers' lab, and Soho Writers' Lab. *These Demons* was longlisted for the 2021 Women's Prize for Playwriting and is her debut play.

JASMINE TEO | DIRECTOR

Jasmine Teo (she/her) is a director who has worked in London and Singapore. She has been involved in the development of *These Demons* since the first draft in 2021. Productions include: *The Bevin Boys* (LPT Standing Ovation Award for Best New Play Raising Awareness 2019), *The Gift* (RADA), *The Art of Charlie Chan Hock Chye* (Pentameters Theatre), *The Last Five Years* (Henderson Project).

Her associate directing credits include: *The Sound of Music* (Chichester Festival Theatre, Adam Penford), *A Christmas Carol* (Bridge Theatre, Sir Nicholas Hytner), *Graceland* (Royal Court, Anna Himali Howard), *A Christmas Carol* (Nottingham Playhouse, Adam Penford). She was Assistant Director on the Olivier-nominated 2022 revival of *Jerusalem*, Baylis Assistant Director on *Camp Siegfried* (Katy Rudd, Old Vic), *The Haystack* (Roxana Silbert, Hampstead Theatre) and *The Wolves* (Ellen McDougall, Theatre Royal Stratford East). Jasmine was a reader for the Old Vic Playwriting for Big Stages Programme and a member of the first Royal Court Directors' Group.

TANYA TRUMAN | CREATIVE PRODUCER

Tanya is both a performer and a creative producer, supported by Stage One. With a particular interest towards both female and Jewish narratives, Tanya has been part of the development of *These Demons* since its first R&D in 2021.

Independent productions include triple OFFIE nominated *Pickle* (Soho Theatre, Park Theatre & Tour), *The Arc: A Trilogy of New Jewish Plays* (Soho Theatre, Co-Production with Emanate Productions), *Fury and Elysium* (The Other Palace Studio), *Becoming Nigella* (In Development - BEAM2023, Oxford Playhouse).

SOPHIE FIRTH | SET & COSTUME DESIGNER

Sophie Firth is a set and costume designer for theatre from London, having graduated from the Royal Academy of Dramatic Arts with a BA (Hons) in Scenic Art and Design in 2022. Since graduating she has worked as both a scenic artist and designer with design credits including *Cinderella and the Forbidden Ball* (OSO Arts Centre), *Hamlet* and *Massacre at Paris* (Fourth Monkey Actor Training Company) the latter of which was co-designed with Anita Gander. Her design credits while in training include *Time and the Conways* (Vanburgh Theatre), *Stop Kiss* (GBS Theatre) and *Consent* (Gielgud Theatre).

SKYLAR TURNBULL HURD | LIGHTING DESIGNER

Skylar (she/her) is a London-based Lighting Designer. She is a graduate from RADA's BA Hons in Technical Theatre and Stage Management, specialising in Lighting Design. Skylar has just been the Assistant Lighting Designer to Jen Schriever on the Broadway transfer of *A Strange Loop* to the Barbican Theatre. She was also the Assistant Lighting Designer to Jon Clark on *Mandela* at the Young Vic. Skylar was the Associate Lighting Designer on *Help! We Are Still Alive* to Lucía Sánchez Roldán at the Seven Dials Playhouse. Earlier this year, Skylar also was Touring Associate Lighting Designer and Relighter on Theatre503's tour of *Tapped* which went to fifteen different venues across the country.

Skylar's lighting designs include: *Looking For Giants* directed by Cesca Echlin at the Camden Peoples' Theatre, *Nice Girls Don't Stay for Breakfast* choreographed by Eleanor McGrath, *Wild Cherries* directed by Kristine Landon-Smith, *NSFW* directed by Joan Oliver.

NIAMH GAFFNEY | SOUND DESIGNER (FOR AUTOGRAPH SOUND)
(She/They)

Training: Graduated LAMDA 2020

Associate Sound Designer credits include; *Cabaret* (KitKatClub Playhouse Theatre 2021, Olivier Award-winner for Best Sound Design 2022), *Bridgerton Secret Cinema* (2022), *Jerusalem* (Apollo Theatre, 2022), *Peaky Blinders Immersive London* (2022), *Secret Cinema Guardians of the Galaxy the Experience* (2022), *Once on This Island* (Regents Park 2023)

Sound Designer: *Pride and Prejudice* (*sort of)* (UK Tour 2022, Olivier Award for Best Entertainment or Comedy 2022).

LAURA WOHLWEND | MOVEMENT DIRECTOR
Laura is a Jewish theatre maker and movement director from Switzerland. She trained on the BA Acting CDT at Royal Central School of Speech and Drama. Laura works as a performer, director and workshop facilitator across the theatre, Motion Capture and film industry in the UK and in France.

Credits as a director and movement director include: *Pickle*, movement director (SOHO Theatre & Park Theatre), *The Dragoness*, director (R&D), *When the Penny Clicks*, director (R&D), *On Cloud Nine*, director (White Bear), *The Power Goes Off*, movement director (The Arcola), *Charlie and the Weather Adventure*, co-director (RHS Wisely, site-specific), *Vernon God Little*, associate director (Royal Central School of Speech and Drama), *Just Lose It*, Bric à Brac assistant director (The Space). Laura has wrapped up filming for two TV shows which will air in 2024 on Disney+ and Amazon.

PEIYAO WANG | COSTUME ASSOCIATE
Peiyao Wang is a recent graduate of The Royal Central School of Speech and Drama. Recent works include *Richard III* (2022) and *Purgatory In Ingolstadt* (2023).

LAUREL MARKS | PRODUCTION MANAGER
Laurel is an Associate Artist of The Jack Studio Theatre, Company Member of Arrows & Traps Theatre Company and Technical Manager of The Hope Theatre.

Production Management credits include: *Past Life* Dir. Maddy Moore (UK Tour), *Tasting Notes* Dir. Shelley Williams (Southwark Playhouse), *The Moors* Dir. Phil Bartlett and *Measured* Dir. Cat Robey (The Hope Theatre).

WAVERLEY MORAN | STAGE MANAGER

Waverley (she/they) traded in sunny Bermuda for rainy England to play pretend for a living. The jury is still out on whether their love of theatre makes up for the lack of beaches in London. Waverley studied Production and Technical Arts at LAMDA and is currently working in Stage Management. She has a particular love for musicals of all kinds, and productions that have diversity and inclusion at the forefront.

Previous work includes Stage Manager of *The Arc: A Trilogy of New Jewish Plays* (Emanate Productions, Soho Theatre), *I Hate it Here* (Sweet Beef Theatre Co.), Assistant Stage Manager of *Two Billion Beats* (Orange Tree Theatre), Deputy Stage Manager of *The Solid Life of Sugar Water* (Orange Tree Theatre), Stage Manager of *Lysistrata* (Lyric Hammersmith), and Stage Manager of *Anyone Can Whistle* (The Grey Area).

LAUREN KOSTER | ASSISTANT DIRECTOR & COVER

Lauren is currently a member of the National Youth Theatre and trains with Mark Jermin.

Theatre includes: *Camp Siegfried* (The Old Vic); *Find Me* (Leatherhead Drama Festival).

Television and short film includes: Unannounced TV series (Netflix); *Mayward Road* (Broken Flames Productions); *I Am Your Sister* (Priddy Productions

BETHANY COOPER | ASSOCIATE PRODUCER

Bethany trained at Theatre503 before setting up Bethany Cooper Productions. BCP produced Katie Redford's debut play *Tapped* (Theatre503) which toured the UK in 2023 and was Offie nominated for Most Promising New Playwright.

Bethany is supported by the Stage One Bursary and the MGCfutures Nicole Kidman Bursary. She is also the Producer for Folio Theatre and a board member for Book, Music & Lyrics. Associate Producer Credits: *The Book Thief* (Belgrade Theatre & Leicester Curve); *The Shape of Things* (The Park Theatre); *Thrones! The Parody Musical* and *Baby Wants Candy* (Edinburgh Fringe Festival). Assistant Producer Credits: *The Fairytale Revolution* (Theatre503).

ACKNOWLEDGEMENTS

The first people to thank are Jasmine Teo and Tanya Truman, who have not only been essential to this play's development but also an endless source of motivation, support, inspiration and snacks. Thank you to the whole Theatre503 team for believing in the script, and to the whole cast and team of this production for throwing yourselves into it.

Thanks also to:

Sensitivity reader Keren David who has offered insight and guidance throughout the different drafts. To the cast and creatives of the two R&Ds who helped us discover the play including Annabel Baldwin, Natasha Karp, Michal Horowicz, Emily Rose Simons, Jida Akil, Rosie Yadid, Beverley Klein, Loren Elstein, Tingying Dong, Anna Short, Lucía Sánchez Roldán, Matt Powell and Sam Lupton. To JW3, and Tsitsit who have supported previous R&Ds and this production. To my Dad, my brother Joel, to Christian and to the rest of my family for putting up with me, and to my Mum who had endless belief in me and would have loved to see this play. To the rabbis who've generously shared their expertise, and to all the friends who have read the script, attended the very much 'in progress' sharings and given their feedback. *These Demons* would not have made it this far without all of you.

R.B.

AUTHOR'S NOTE

The idea for this play began with a realisation; demons exist within Judaism.

I came across this fact accidentally while trawling through Google for a totally different play I was working on. I wanted to know why no one I knew had told me about them, and quickly learned that this was because my family and Jewish friends hadn't heard about them either. The original play didn't quite work, but the concept of Jewish demonology stuck with me.

I spoke to a rabbi from my local synagogue, who pointed me to extracts in the Talmud referring to a type of demon called the *mazzikim*, and said that although demons are a small part of some key religious texts, we rarely like to talk about them. A couple years later, it was still on my mind. The idea evolved into a story that wove together different demons from little-known strands of Jewish ideology and history. It became a story about family and identity, the ideas and fears we suppress, and fear of the otherness inside others and in ourselves.

Why am I telling you this? I guess I want to say that, while I'm no expert in the subject matter, the demons in this play are not made up. At the same time, it feels somehow important to clarify that demons and exorcisms are not part of mainstream Judaism today.

I've tried to be accurate, respectful and sensitive, working with Jewish and global majority creatives throughout the development process. Inevitably there are many different interpretations of these ideas, just as there are many different lived experiences that we have and haven't touched on. I hope that the story nevertheless speaks to you in some way, and that it says something just a little helpful or interesting about acceptance of our differences, and embracing the things we don't or can't understand.

CHARACTERS

LEAH – seventeen

DANIELLE – twenty-two

MIRAH – late forties or early fifties

SETTING

The events of the play take place in a cottage, two hours outside London.

Scenes can bleed into one another, and reality distorts as the play goes on.

TIME

Now.

NOTES ON TEXT

/ Slashes indicate overlapping dialogue.

– Dashes indicate an interruption.

, A comma on its own line indicates a short beat, or a shift in tone or thought.

ACT I

Scene One

(A small English cottage. Rustic and cluttered.)

(Beside the cottage, an overgrown garden.)

(Surrounding the garden, woods. Leaves cover the ground.)

(It's late afternoon.)

(Inside, books are piled on every surface.)

(On a shelf is an old-fashioned radio. Behind it, a tarnished Channukia.)

(One of the walls is covered in scribbled Post-it notes and pieces of paper.)

(In full view is a window; glass cracked, lines emanating from a central point as if something has flown into it. A rock? A bird?)

*(**LEAH** has been adding to the Post-it wall, flicking through books, searching for something. Finally, she finds the page she wants and reads out loud.)*

LEAH. "If the eye had the power to see them, no creature could endure the *mazzikim*. They are more numerous than we are and they surround us like a ridge around a field."

>	*(Pausing, trying to work something out, then reading again.)*

LEAH.	"If the eye had the power to see them, no creature could endure the *mazzikim*. They are more numerous than we are and they surround us like a ridge around a field. Every one among us has a thousand on his left hand and ten thousand on his right hand..."

>	*(A sudden, loud noise from inside the cottage. Something falling to the floor.* **LEAH** *is startled and goes to investigate. We are alone.)*

>	*(The broken window shudders.)*

>	*(***LEAH*** *returns and sees the window. It is still.)*

>	*(Another noise, this time from outside. A car parking.* **LEAH** *can't see out the back, so she picks up a large kitchen knife and waits facing the door.)*

>	*(Unseen by* **LEAH**, **DANIELLE** *approaches the front door from outside. She takes an anxious breath, then enters.)*

DANIELLE.	Jesus hell almighty Christ on a bike!

LEAH.	Danielle?

DANIELLE.	What have you got that / for?

LEAH.	How did / you find me?

DANIELLE.	You gave me a literal heart attack.

LEAH.	Speak for yourself.

DANIELLE.	No but I mean seriously, seriously will you please put that down?

>	*(They both stare at the knife in* **LEAH**'s *hand. She lowers it onto the table.)*

LEAH.	What are you doing here?

DANIELLE. What are *you* doing here? Is this where you've been the whole time?

LEAH. You weren't meant to follow me.

DANIELLE. Leah! We've been looking for you.

,

You went missing?

LEAH. *(Shrugging.)* Obvs not.

DANIELLE. You didn't come home last night. You weren't in school. If I hadn't found you here we would've... Dad agreed we'd call the police.

LEAH. That's a bit dramatic.

DANIELLE. Is it though? I mean, did you think we wouldn't notice?

LEAH. Dad's at his conference in Birmingham.

DANIELLE. Exactly. It was just me. I'm responsible.

LEAH. Well I didn't think you'd...

DANIELLE. What?

LEAH. Nothing. Okay. Care.

DANIELLE. Leah!

LEAH. Well do you?

*(A beat. **DANIELLE** looks away.)*

DANIELLE. I missed work to look for you.

LEAH. You did?

DANIELLE. I told them I was feeling sick. I missed half the afternoon.

LEAH. Oh no half the afternoon.

DANIELLE. I've not taken a sick day since Year Nine.

LEAH. Well. It's only an internship.

DANIELLE. Grad scheme.

LEAH. Bet the corporate machine had a breakdown.

DANIELLE. It's not a corporate machine. It's John Lewis.

> (**LEAH** *makes a face.*)

Can we go? Put your shoes on. This place smells like
cat food.

> (**LEAH** *does nothing.*)

If we leave now, and if I drive as fast as I can without
breaking the speed limit, I think we'll make it home for
Bake Off.

> (*At the door.*)

Vamos.

LEAH. I'm not going.

DANIELLE. Yes you are.

LEAH. Nope.

DANIELLE. Excuse me, what?

LEAH. I'm not leaving because you tell me to.

DANIELLE. Excuse me what?

LEAH. You just said that twice.

DANIELLE. But...

LEAH. I'm staying.

> (**DANIELLE** *takes a deep breath in, then out.*)

DANIELLE. Why? What are you actually doing here?

,   .

I mean really. I mean, is that your handwriting?

> (*She moves towards the notes on the wall.*)

Are those yours?

(**LEAH** *rushes to block her view.*)

LEAH. Doesn't matter.

DANIELLE. But what –

LEAH. It's nothing.

DANIELLE. Nothing?

LEAH. If you want to go so badly, go. I don't care.

DANIELLE. Leah. I didn't drive for two hours, in rush hour traffic, to this shithole in the middle of nowhere, just to turn around and leave without you.

LEAH. It's not a shithole.

DANIELLE. Look at it. I mean, Jesus. I haven't been here since she moved in. Dad said the house was falling down, but.

(*She inspects the room and recoils.*)

Is Aunt Mirah just a slob, or is she, you know, losing it?

LEAH. Take that back.

DANIELLE. No. Actually, okay. If you come home with me right now.

LEAH. I told you I can't.

DANIELLE. Oh you can. You just won't.

,

You know what? Whatever this is, you can explain it to Dad.

(*Getting out her phone.*) That way he can tell you to do what you're told, and we can leave, and...and...

(**DANIELLE** *fumbles with her phone for a good while.*)

LEAH. There's no signal.

,

There's not even wifi half the time.

DANIELLE. But...

LEAH. Mirah has to do online lectures sometimes. Drives her nuts.

(**DANIELLE** *moves towards the landline.*)

Landline's been broken since I got here. It used to work, but.

(**DANIELLE** *tries it anyway.*)

I mean it. I tried ordering pizza, but, no pizza. A short tragedy.

DANIELLE. How do I tell Dad you're not floating in some ditch?

LEAH. He doesn't think that.

DANIELLE. How would you know?

LEAH. It's dumped in a ditch or floating in a river.

,

Plus the body would be weighted. Unless my killer was doing that test to see if I would float. Like if they thought I was a witch, or just. Really gassy.

DANIELLE. We'll have to drive to somewhere with signal, to tell him you're okay, otherwise he'll freak out.

LEAH. No, you'll freak out. Besides, if I get in the car with you...

DANIELLE. Yes?

LEAH. You'll kidnap me.

DANIELLE. I don't think it counts as kidnapping if I'm your sister. Like, legally, I'm not sure it counts.

LEAH. But you admit you'll make me go home?

   (*Pause.*)

DANIELLE. Tell me what's going on.

LEAH. …

DANIELLE. I'm serious.

LEAH. I'm getting that. You're acting proper weird.

DANIELLE. Me? You're the one who's… Why are you here?

LEAH. Maybe I'm here to feed Babs.

DANIELLE. The cat?

LEAH. She's Barbara to you. Babs if you're a friend.

DANIELLE. Will you just stop. What are those notes you're making?

   ,

   I called the school this morning. Since you never came home. They said you weren't there, but your Head of Sixth Form wasn't even surprised. Apparently bunking off is normal for you.

LEAH. I'm not here to bunk off.

DANIELLE. Dad messaged me the names of your friends. They were freaked I was even texting. Sophie said you hadn't hung out since Year Ten.

LEAH. Dad's out of date.

DANIELLE. That's when I left work. I went back home, to see if your passport was there. To see if maybe / you'd –

LEAH. It was there.

DANIELLE. Yes, but I wanted to see / if –

LEAH. I didn't jet off to Ibiza.

DANIELLE. I wanted to see if you'd gone to visit Mum.

(Unseen by both of them, a feather falls from the ceiling.)

LEAH. Obviously not.

DANIELLE. No. Obviously not.

,

Then, I tried calling Aunt Mirah.

LEAH. How'd that go?

DANIELLE. She didn't pick up.

LEAH. Do you know why she didn't pick up? It wasn't 'cause of bad wifi.

DANIELLE. Why didn't she pick –

LEAH. 'Cause she's in hospital.

DANIELLE. In hospital? Is she okay?

LEAH. She is now.

(There's a faint sound, like a scuttle.)

She fractured her kneecap. I was the one who found her yesterday.

DANIELLE. Found her?

,

Were you bunking off yesterday too?

LEAH. Did you hear what I said?

DANIELLE. Is this where you go? Does Aunt Mirah let you just –

LEAH. Did you hear what I –

DANIELLE. Yes. You said she fell.

LEAH. She didn't just fall.

DANIELLE. What do you mean?

LEAH. She's not an old lady. She didn't go to A&E in an ambulance 'cause she 'fell'.

DANIELLE. Okay. Then –

LEAH. Someone hurt her on purpose.

DANIELLE. Hang on, what?

LEAH. That's why I'm back here. Because I had to do something.

,

I know who hurt Aunt Mirah. By the time I found her yesterday, he'd already left.

DANIELLE. Wait, who?

LEAH. So I came back last night. I decided to send him a message.

DANIELLE. You what?

LEAH. A note. I stuck one up in the newsagents this morning. And the pub.

DANIELLE. You left notes, like physically?

LEAH. Also the church.

DANIELLE. The church?

LEAH. Just on the door. He'll know it's for him.

DANIELLE. Hang on, wait. Wait, wait, wait. Who's 'him'?

(Time starts to shift.)

Scene Two

(Now – continuous / Two months ago.)

*(***LEAH*** *continues speaking as if* ***DANIELLE*** *is still listening in the present.)*

LEAH. The boy came here once before. Two months ago. I was here for Shabbat.

*(***MIRAH*** *enters and sets the scene.)*

Couple prayers. Super out of date kosher wine. Shit pasta.

*(***MIRAH*** *puts a bowl of pasta in front of* ***LEAH***.*)*

Aunt Mirah and I were talking about... Well, normal stuff.

MIRAH. Sixteenth February, Fifteen Seventy-One: The Great Event in Tzfat!

*(***LEAH*** *turns to* ***MIRAH***, *now inside the scene from two months ago.)*

LEAH. Tz-what?

MIRAH. A city in Israel.

LEAH. Oh.

MIRAH. Not like Israel now. That is not the point of this story. Listen. Eat.

*(***LEAH*** *takes a bite of pasta.)*

Good. Now. Fifteen Seventy-One. The night was / dark –

LEAH. It's undercooked.

MIRAH. The night was –

LEAH. You al-totally-dente'd it.

MIRAH. Chew with your mouth closed, you harpy.

,

Fifteen Seventy-One. More than one hundred men were gathered. Torah scholars, heads of communities. They were there to witness a young woman. A girl who had been – so the accounts say – possessed. By a demon. Later writings would class it as a *Dybbuk*.

LEAH. Which one's that?

MIRAH. A possessive demon, obviously. *Dybbuk*. Translation: 'to cling'.

,

Two men approached, each knowledgeable about spirit possession. And so they began the exorcism.

LEAH. Wait –

MIRAH. Don't speak with your mouth full.

LEAH. Jews don't do exorcisms.

MIRAH. Leah. You're telling me you don't know the steps to a sixteenth-century Jewish exorcism? What the fuck did they teach you at *Cheder*? Alright, pay attention. Step One!

LEAH. Step One…

MIRAH. Question the demon.

LEAH. About what? His favourite pasta?

MIRAH. You could try to ask if it has a name, the nature of its sins, how it entered the body of the possessed.

LEAH. Mine's spaghetti hoops.

(*Beat.*)

MIRAH. I thought you said you wanted to hear about my new book, but if I'm boring you then –

LEAH. Sorry. Yes. Please

MIRAH. To encourage the demon to answer, you might recite incantations. And that is exactly what the men in Tzfat did:

(*Reciting in Hebrew.*)

יֹשֵׁב, בְּסֵתֶר עֶלְיוֹן;   בְּצֵל שַׁדַּי, יִתְלוֹנָן
(*yo·shev be·se·ter el·yo·n; be·tzel shadai yit·lo·nan.*)

אֹמַר—לַיהוָה, מַחְסִי וּמְצוּדָתִי;   אֱלֹהַי, אֶבְטַח-בּוֹ
(*o·mar la·shem mach·si u·me·tzu·da·ti; e·lo·hai ev·tach-bo.*)

Psalm ninety-one.

LEAH. Did it work?

MIRAH. It did not. And so, they proceeded to Step Two: Fumigation. Fire, smoke and sulphur.

LEAH. Sulphur. Isn't that –

MIRAH. Eggy. Like an omelette that wants to kill you.

LEAH. I was gonna say poisonous. We learnt that in Chemistry.

MIRAH. Oh yes, the fumes were highly toxic. But the two men held the girl down, to make the smoke enter her nostrils. The account says that she would not move away, even from the flames. But then, suddenly, all who were gathered heard a voice. Like "the voice of the Almighty". Drawn out like a rooooaaar!

LEAH. So, the girl was screaming?

MIRAH. The account describes the men having a conversation with the demon.

LEAH. While they were torturing her?

MIRAH. Smoking her. Like a Scottish salmon. And the two men begged the spirit: "Please. Please leave. Leave this young woman alone!" That is the next step: to demand that the demon go away.

(Lowering her voice.) I must warn you, this demand comes with great danger. If you're not careful, the demon will leave through an organ. Sometimes, the throat. If you're not careful, it will choke you.

LEAH. ...Is that what happened?

MIRAH. Traditionally, the way to tell if an exorcism has worked is if a candle blows out. And if it hasn't blown out, the traditional way to make the demon leave is to force it out through the toe.

LEAH. What? Cut it off?

MIRAH. The big toenail.

LEAH. Cut off the toenail? Who decided that?

MIRAH. It's the customary exorcism method.

LEAH. *(Very into the gore.)* Was there loads of blood?

MIRAH. And not just from the toe. Guess.

LEAH. Ooh, um, ooh, maybe –

MIRAH. The spirit departed through her vagina.

LEAH. ...You made that up.

MIRAH. That's what the original account says. Why the men were looking, I, uh, well...

LEAH. *(Pushing away her bowl.)* Don't want this anymore.

MIRAH. No? Remind me to read more about exorcisms next time I'm on a diet.

LEAH. Remind me to go to dinner at yours next time I'm on a diet.

(**MIRAH** *takes Leah's bowl.*)

MIRAH. Don't want it? Don't deserve it.

LEAH. I'll tell my Dad you don't feed me.

MIRAH. No you won't, or he'll stop you coming here. Sounds quite peaceful actually.

LEAH. You make better food for Barbara.

MIRAH. Babs appreciates what she gets, unlike you.

>*(There's a noise outside, a kind of crash. **LEAH** runs to the window.)*

Well that's not Babs.

LEAH. Hey. Hey!

MIRAH. Is it a fox?

LEAH. It's a boy.

>*(**MIRAH** goes to the window as **LEAH** shouts.)*

Hey. Get out!

MIRAH. Don't.

LEAH. But he's emptying your bins all over the garden!

,

I'm going after him.

MIRAH. You will not.

LEAH. But he's basically my age. I can take him. I did self-defence.

MIRAH. An after-school club won't cut it. Please, I'm trying to stay out of village politics.

,

MIRAH. I mean it. Let's wait for him to leave.

LEAH. But –

MIRAH. No buts.

>*(They wait, watching through the window...)*

LEAH. He's gone.

(**LEAH** *runs into the garden.* **MIRAH** *follows.*)

MIRAH. If you don't mind helping.

(**MIRAH** *starts picking rubbish off the ground.*)

LEAH. I don't get it.

MIRAH.   There's a group of them from the village. Teenagers. Was it just the one boy?

LEAH. Yeah, just the one.

(**LEAH** *begins to help.*)

MIRAH. They've never come out here before.

LEAH. Do you know who he was?

MIRAH. Not personally.

LEAH. Can you report him?

MIRAH. To who? I don't know who this kid's parents are, but they probably know me. And I'm not exactly... I'm not in the WhatsApp group, put it that way.

,

He didn't bring a car either.

LEAH. So he walked here? Through the woods? That's nuts.

MIRAH. You do it every month.

LEAH. I like the river. And you give me food. Kind of.

MIRAH. Maybe if you gave me more notice about when you'd show up, I'd get other food in. Or offer you a lift, or even –

(**MIRAH** *stops sharply, staring at the ground.*)

LEAH. Even what?

MIRAH. You go over there, by the gate. I'll clear the rock garden.

LEAH. But what –

MIRAH. It doesn't matter.

LEAH. Has he written something? In the dirt?

> *(Trying to block **LEAH**'s view, **MIRAH** covers up the message in the mud.)*

MIRAH. I can clear the rest of this later, actually.

,

Shall we go inside for pudding? Something else to encourage your diet?

LEAH. Are you not going to tell me what he wrote?

> *(Pause.)*

MIRAH. Do you know, after the exorcism, the girl died.

LEAH. What?

MIRAH. The Great Event in Tzfat. Fifteen Seventy-One. Eight days after the exorcism, she choked.

LEAH. ...Oh.

MIRAH. There are two main theories. One is that the men smoked her to death. That would be the most logical explanation.

LEAH. ...What's the other?

MIRAH. In the account, some witnesses said that the candle never blew out. What that 'could' suggest, is that the demon never left.

Scene Three

(Now. **DANIELLE** *is still with* **LEAH** *in the cottage.* **LEAH***'s described what we've just seen.)*

DANIELLE. So. What did he write?

LEAH. What do you mean?

DANIELLE. The message that kid wrote in the dirt?

LEAH. He's not a kid, he looked my age.

DANIELLE. But what did it say?

,

I mean, what does it have to do with yesterday. I'm trying to understand here.

(A beat.)

LEAH. It said –

DANIELLE. Are you even sure it was the same guy?

LEAH. Mirah told me.

DANIELLE. Okay. So –

LEAH. Are you saying Aunt Mirah's a liar?

DANIELLE. No. No...

LEAH. When I went with her to hospital, she said there's a group of them in the village – teenagers – who've been making her uncomfortable. She said the same boy who messed with her bins came back and threw a rock at her window. That window.

*(***DANIELLE*** goes to the broken window.)*

DANIELLE. Uncomfortable how?

LEAH. Mirah wouldn't say.

DANIELLE. Right.

(Looking at the window.)

DANIELLE. It didn't break.

LEAH. So?

DANIELLE. So how hard did this boy throw the rock?

LEAH. What does it matter? Maybe he's a crap thrower.

DANIELLE. But why was it just him? Just one of the group?

LEAH. He's a shitbag?

DANIELLE. But... You said he hurt Aunt Mirah?

LEAH. She went out to have a go at him. 'Cause he'd just smashed up her window.

DANIELLE. Okay. And then?

LEAH. Then, she fractured her kneecap. On the rock garden. When I found her she'd tried to numb it with ibuprofen, that's it.

,

What?

DANIELLE. Why didn't you tell me? You could have called.

LEAH. I was busy going with her to hospital.

DANIELLE. But –

LEAH. Plus you were at your precious job.

DANIELLE. But... If she didn't fall, then, what? He pushed her?

LEAH. He clearly meant to hurt her.

DANIELLE. Is that what Aunt Mirah thinks? Is she reporting it?

LEAH. No.

,

But –

DANIELLE. Why would a teenager hurt a middle-aged woman? That's just embarrassing. What's his problem?

LEAH. I don't know, do I? I mean, I do… The message in the dirt.

DANIELLE. Yes?

LEAH. It said…

,

,

It said "Fuck off you Jewish witch."

(Long pause.)

DANIELLE. Right.

,

I mean, it could have been worse.

LEAH. Are you fucking kidding?

DANIELLE. Okay, sorry. I mean, yes, it could have been worse. She is Jewish.

LEAH. Danielle!

DANIELLE. And…and she has a cat.

LEAH. Danielle!

DANIELLE. No but I'm being serious. She chose to move out here, didn't she? She chose to leave the place where she was one of millions, and where she could get every Deliveroo imaginable, to go live in a place with thatched roofs. I drove through that high street earlier, and I didn't even realise it was the high street.

LEAH. What's your point?

DANIELLE. All I saw was the church.

,

Has she even been inside the church?

,

DANIELLE. If you're going to move somewhere like this, at least...at least try to integrate.

LEAH. You don't know what you're on about.

DANIELLE. At least I've lived outside of London.

LEAH. Isn't Durham Uni basically London?

DANIELLE. I joined the choir. I sang in the carol service. All my friends did.

LEAH. Ding Dong Merrily on High.

DANIELLE. It was actually fun.

LEAH. So you like blending in. Like a stick insect.

DANIELLE. No –

LEAH. You're saying that maybe Aunt Mirah wouldn't have been attacked if she'd joined a choir?

DANIELLE. What I'm saying is, she's out here, in the woods, writing about demons and mystic Jewish rituals. That doesn't look... Even for average Jews, that's not normal.

> (*A faint scuttling begins.* **DANIELLE**, *unaware of this, reads from the shelves.*)

'Lilith: Woman, Mother or Demon?' 'Exorcisms through the Male Gaze'. Jesus, Leah, that's not what Judaism's about.

LEAH. I don't think carols are very average Jew either, so.

DANIELLE. But this stuff is so...so weird.

LEAH. Those books are bestsellers.

DANIELLE. One was a bestseller. Sort of. I mean look. She's framed a press cutting from twelve years ago. It's pretty cringe.

LEAH. You're being mean.

DANIELLE. It's not mean if it's facts. Dad would agree. Mum would agree.

LEAH. Mum has nothing to do with this.

>   *(Beat.)*

Anyway Mirah hasn't spoken to her in years.

DANIELLE. And why do you think Aunt Mirah and Mum haven't spoken?

>   ,

Look, I'm just saying that sometimes Mirah stands out deliberately. And even if what happened yesterday wasn't an accident... I'm not saying she was asking for it. But, maybe she was asking for it.

>   *(There's a creak from within the cottage.)*

LEAH. Who even are you?

DANIELLE. I just mean, if what happened yesterday is as bad as you think, why isn't Aunt Mirah telling anyone? Did you ask?

LEAH. She said she doesn't want to make it a 'thing' in the village. She doesn't want to get the police involved.

DANIELLE. Why not?

LEAH. All it means is there's no proof.

DANIELLE. Okay. Maybe, if she doesn't feel safe here anymore, maybe she shouldn't live here.

>   ,

What?

LEAH. You were the one saying what happened was nothing.

DANIELLE. I said it could have been worse. There's a difference.

>   *(Beat.)*

LEAH. So that's your answer? If you don't fit in, get out?

DANIELLE. I don't have answers. I'm just. Using common sense.

LEAH. But that's exactly why I'm here.

DANIELLE. What do you mean?

LEAH. To make it right.

,

What happened was a hate crime. Right now there's no proof. But if I can find the boy, and get him to admit what he did – and why he did it – then there'd be evidence.

DANIELLE. Excuse me what?

LEAH. That's why I left notes round the village. This place is tiny. It'll work.

DANIELLE. Wait wait wait – what will 'work'?

LEAH. If I can get him alone, then / I can –

DANIELLE. Oh, no. No no no, that is not a good idea.

LEAH. I'm going to talk to him, and record it. Then I'll have evidence.

DANIELLE. Christ, record it like on your phone? Like post it on your loser TikTok?

LEAH. I knew you wouldn't get it.

DANIELLE. This boy is obviously, obviously dangerous.

LEAH. I don't think he's very smart.

DANIELLE. You can be stupid and dangerous at the same time.

,

Have you considered that he will beat you to a pulp?

LEAH. If he does, then I'll be the evidence.

DANIELLE. That's not funny.

LEAH. If you don't want to be part of this, don't watch. But don't try to control me.

DANIELLE. What do you mean, watch?

(Realising.) You asked him to come here?

,

We have to go. Now. Get your things.

,

This is worse than I thought. This is just. You've lost it. You've actually lost it. I don't deserve this... I'm calling Dad. I'm calling Dad, and...

LEAH. No signal.

DANIELLE. Put your shoes on right now.

LEAH. Or what?

DANIELLE. Or...I won't speak to you again.

> *(Beat.)*

LEAH. Sweet.

DANIELLE. Leah I'm being serious.

> *(**DANIELLE** tries to grab **LEAH** and lead her to the door.)*

LEAH. Get off me!

> *(**LEAH** smacks **DANIELLE**'s shoulder, struggling out of her grip.)*

I told you I'm staying here.

> *(**DANIELLE** fights to stay calm.)*

DANIELLE. That actually hurt.

,

Is that why you had the knife earlier? Because you thought it might have been him at the door?

*(**LEAH** finds the knife and picks it up.)*

LEAH. This knife?

DANIELLE. Put that down.

LEAH. Why? If I was chopping an avocado you wouldn't care.

DANIELLE. What the hell do you think he'll do when he sees you with a weapon?

LEAH. It's not like I'm going to use it.

DANIELLE. He doesn't know that. Besides, what if you lose your temper, and…and…

LEAH. What do you mean lose my temper?

(Angry.) I never lose my temper!

DANIELLE. Dad told me that the school said you sometimes get…emotional.

LEAH. Fuck school. They're lying. One time, okay? One time, I got angry, but that was years ago.

DANIELLE. So prove it – stop waving that around. Stop scaring me.

LEAH. Obviously you have to make this about you.

DANIELLE. Trust me, if I was thinking about me right now, I'd have left.

*(The radio switches on, humming with a low static. **LEAH** still holds the knife.)*

LEAH. That's what you do, isn't it. When things get too much.

DANIELLE. Put that down I swear to god.

LEAH. You leave, or you boss me around.

DANIELLE. Jesus. Will you turn off that noise?

LEAH. See, bossing me about again. You act like you never care about anything, and then you go and…

(Realising.) I didn't turn on the radio.

> **(LEAH** *tries to turn it off, but the static continues.)*

I didn't turn it on.

DANIELLE. This isn't funny.

> **(LEAH** *unplugs the radio. It makes no difference.)*

LEAH. What's it doing? Do you hear that noise?

> *(She looks frantically about the room.)*

DANIELLE. Leah...

LEAH. I've been hearing things since I got here.

DANIELLE. It's just broken.

LEAH. Other sounds. Like a...scuttling. Have you heard it?

> *(She picks up a book.)*

"If the eye had the power to see them, no creature could endure the *mazzikim*."

DANIELLE. What?

LEAH. It's a quote from the Talmud.

'

It's a text of Jewish law from / the year –

DANIELLE. I know what the Talmud is. What are you on about?

LEAH. I have this theory. About the noises. I've never heard them before.

DANIELLE. It's just static. The radio.

LEAH. I don't mean the radio.

DANIELLE. Stand still. I need you to breathe. Count. In through the nose. Out through the mouth.

LEAH. Stop talking to me like that.

DANIELLE. I'll stop when we leave.

LEAH. You don't understand. I'm not leaving.

> (**DANIELLE** *tries to drag* **LEAH** *towards the door.*)
>
> (*A figure – made up of shadows – takes shape. It looks like a figure with wings.*)
>
> (*The two sisters grapple with each other, until, with determination,* **LEAH** *holds the knife to her palm and cuts it open.*)

ACT II

Scene One

(Now – a space here and not here.)

*(**LEAH**'s hand is bleeding.)*

LEAH. Danielle!

*(But **DANIELLE** isn't here.)*

(This doesn't feel real.)

Danielle!

*(**LEAH** stares at the blood.)*

I didn't mean to. I don't know why I... I didn't mean it.

MIRAH. *(Offstage.)* Here we go!

LEAH. *(Confused.)* What?

(Time shifts.)

Scene Two

> (*Two years ago.* **MIRAH** *enters from the hallway holding a shoebox.* **LEAH** *stares at her injured hand.*)

MIRAH. This will be painful as hell but it will do the trick.

> (**LEAH** *sees the shoebox.*)

LEAH. What's that?

MIRAH. Arnica. It will reduce the swelling.

LEAH. Is that one of your fake medicines?

MIRAH. It's herbal, yes. Hand?

> (**MIRAH** *applies the gel. Her approach is practical rather than gentle.*)

MIRAH. So you were just passing through the woods at one o'clock on a Tuesday, by coincidence?

LEAH. Why not?

MIRAH. I might live under a rock, but even I know you're meant to be in school.

'

If you're going to turn up unannounced instead of doing your GCSEs, at least tell me why.

LEAH. Exams aren't for like a year. Plus all I'm missing's Geography. That's not even a real subject.

MIRAH. Is it not?

LEAH. Not in Year Ten. The best part's the trip to go look at mud.

MIRAH. Well. Don't bunk off school again without telling me first. I'm guessing your Dad doesn't know you're here?

LEAH. Don't tell him.

MIRAH. Now you want me to keep secrets for you?

LEAH. ...Yes?

MIRAH. Hmm.

LEAH. Dad wouldn't get it. But I thought you... I hoped... Please?

MIRAH. *(Relenting, unable to resist.)* If you missed lunch I have frozen pizza. You can use it as an ice pack or eat it, your choice.

LEAH. I'm good. Thanks.

MIRAH. So, what happened?

> ,

You'll feel better if you talk about it.

LEAH. It was just people at school.

MIRAH. Of course it was.

LEAH. They started it.

MIRAH. Tell me, who's 'they'?

LEAH. In PE we have to wear these tiny stupid skirts. The teacher put us in the sports hall with the boys, 'cause it rained. Everyone was looking at me, laughing.

MIRAH. Are you sure they were laughing at you?

LEAH. That's how it felt.

> ,

Then I tripped and hurt my hand.

MIRAH. You tripped?

LEAH. Okay, I punched Callum's nose. Blood everywhere. Best shot of the game.

> (**LEAH** *expected a laugh, but instead* **MIRAH** *grows quiet.)*

LEAH. He deserved it. He did!

MIRAH. So you lost your temper.

LEAH. He pushed me first. Not that anyone saw.

,

What?

MIRAH. Were you hoping I'd say "well done"?

LEAH. I will have that pizza actually.

MIRAH. No. You can't. You behaved like a feral cat.

    (**LEAH** *hisses at* **MIRAH**.)

So you ran here because you thought I'd go easy on you?

LEAH. All I'd get at home is Dad saying I'm wasting my potential. "Danielle never got in trouble. Be more like Danielle." Blah blah, she gets to live in a castle learning about business and being so boring her whole personality is being vegan. And a dick. Besides, I'm already... you know.

MIRAH. Grounded?

LEAH. Suspended. I'm suspended.

,

Say something.

MIRAH. Fuck.

,

Sorry, did you want me to help you feel better? You asked the wrong woman.

    (*A moment between them. Whose side is* **MIRAH** *on?*)

I won't tell your Dad. But you have to promise not to do this again.

LEAH. Can't bunk off if I'm suspended.

MIRAH. I mean lash out at people. Even if they bully you.

LEAH. But Callum's the one who started it, even though everyone took his side. It's not fair.

MIRAH. But the thing is that doesn't matter.

LEAH. But –

MIRAH. People talk even when it's not fair. Rumours, lies. I should know.

LEAH. Wait, you're saying there'll be rumours about me, at school?

,

Shit. Oh shit.

MIRAH. No. That's not what I meant.

LEAH. But it's true. Kill me now.

MIRAH. But that isn't why you shouldn't lash out. You can't control him, but you can control the way you react. Behaviour like that can become a habit. It can fester, and become part of you. It's like...

> (**MIRAH** *picks up a book from one of the shelves.*)

There's a tradition that says demons can be created by our deeds. It works both ways; when we do something good, it creates an angel. When we do something bad it creates...well, there you go.

> (*A beat.*)

LEAH. This is one of your books, isn't it.

MIRAH. I didn't make it up. It's part of *Kabbalah.* A school of Jewish mysticism.

> (**MIRAH** *hands the book to* **LEAH.**)

LEAH. Your first book?

MIRAH. My bestseller, thank you very much.

LEAH. So. If doing bad things makes demons, the sports hall is demonic as hell.

MIRAH. Think of it as the energy you put into the world.

LEAH. So, next time, I'll punch Callum's nose in my head.

MIRAH. But a 'deed' doesn't have to be an act. It can also be a thought.

LEAH. Ugh.

MIRAH. Or a wish. And your demons are personal. Only you can see them. They end up punishing you.

LEAH. That's no fun.

MIRAH. It's not a mainstream idea.

LEAH. But this book's the one that was, like, successful.

MIRAH. The 'one'. As if 'success' can be defined by – okay yes fine. It helped pay for this house, if that's what you mean.

LEAH. Danielle says Madonna helped.

MIRAH. That is an overstatement.

LEAH. But Danielle said –

MIRAH. The celebrity version of Kabbalah was in vogue, briefly. Nothing like my version, but it made people interested in what I had to say.

LEAH. You got rich.

MIRAH. Please, show me my riches. I'll use it to fix the boiler.

,

Of course some people said I was selling out, using my religion to make money.

LEAH. People said that?

MIRAH. Back home, yes. Before I moved here. Some questioned what right I had to publish when I wasn't even... I love being Jewish. Of course I do. I've spent my life studying it. But for a few people, I still wasn't Jewish enough. I wasn't 'in' with the community.

LEAH. I hope you punched them in the nose.

MIRAH. But you see, I learned to control the way I behaved.

,

Besides, I can take judgement from strangers. What I found hardest was when the people who knew me best didn't stand up for me. Your Mum and Dad, for example. They made it clear what they thought.

LEAH. Did they?

MIRAH. No. Yes. I shouldn't tell you.

,

It was in what they didn't say. By letting others talk. I remember once at synagogue, someone asked about my book. Poking fun, and not in a nice way. Your Mum was there, and I thought she might step in, but of course she was silent... And I remember thinking, "If I'm an outsider here I may as well be an outsider somewhere else." I think when I moved, everyone at home was secretly relieved.

,

But that was years ago, and as you can see I don't hold grudges.

LEAH. Well I think it's cool. You out here. "Lone woman in the woods." You don't need anyone else.

MIRAH. Is that what you think?

LEAH. Well yeah. I mean, you don't have to deal with family crap.

MIRAH. No. Except for you.

LEAH. That's what I want to do, when I finish school. I'll go to the middle of nowhere. Live alone. No way do I want children.

MIRAH. You might change your mind.

LEAH. Why? You didn't.

> (**MIRAH** *turns away, trying to hide that this hurts.)*

I'm saying that's cool.

MIRAH. It does seem to be how I ended up.

LEAH. What do you mean?

MIRAH. I was being flippant about being the outsider. I didn't plan on being the old witch in the woods.

LEAH. I didn't say witch.

MIRAH. It doesn't matter.

,

Leave it. Shall I see about that pizza?

LEAH. *(An inkling she's hit a nerve.)* Yeah... So, I can stay? For the afternoon I mean.

MIRAH. If you're good.

> (**MIRAH** *leaves, heading to the kitchen. As she goes, we hear* **DANIELLE** *calling from offstage...)*

Scene Three

(Now.)

DANIELLE. *(Offstage.)* I thought you said under the stairs?

> *(It's dusk. Some time after **LEAH** cut her hand. **LEAH** picks up a tea towel and drapes it around the wound.)*

> *(There's a crash. The sound of falling boxes.)*

(Offstage.) Christ.

LEAH. Can you see a shoebox?

> *(**LEAH** picks up the book that **MIRAH** gave her in the previous scene, and starts flicking through, comparing it to the notes on the wall.)*

> *(**DANIELLE** emerges carrying a pile of shoeboxes.)*

DANIELLE. It's like a cupboard that takes you back in time. I think I saw a bag from Woolworths. Like Narnia, but worse.

> ,

How's it feel?

LEAH. I mean. It hurts.

DANIELLE. Is it still bleeding?

LEAH. Um...

DANIELLE. I think you're meant to keep the pressure until it stops.

LEAH. You should've been a surgeon.

DANIELLE. Will you let me?

> *(Gently, **DANIELLE** presses the tea towel against **LEAH**'s palm.)*

DANIELLE. Tell me if it hurts more.

LEAH. It doesn't.

>   *(They wait for a while.)*

DANIELLE. Oh hang on, was this tea towel clean? I mean to begin with?

LEAH. I think that's a ketchup stain.

>   ,

Could be soup. Could be cat vom. Will I get infected?

DANIELLE. Wash it again. And use soap.

LEAH. But that stings.

DANIELLE. Meanwhile an infection will feel like getting a massage.

>   ,

Please wash it? I'll keep looking for this first-aid shoebox.

>   *(Reluctantly **LEAH** leaves, heading towards the kitchen.)*

>   *(Alone, **DANIELLE** starts looking through the book **LEAH** was reading, and the notes on the wall.)*

>   *(As **LEAH** returns **DANIELLE** goes back to the boxes.)*

LEAH. Hot water's gone. Also I remembered. First-aid's the blue one.

DANIELLE. Oh, good. All I found were these old reviews.

LEAH. From Mirah's books? Can I see?

DANIELLE. First, let me sort your hand.

LEAH. Boring.

>   *(**DANIELLE** takes a bandage out of the box.)*

DANIELLE. Here we are.

LEAH. If you cut off my circulation –

DANIELLE. Oh shush.

> (**LEAH** *waits as* **DANIELLE** *wraps the bandage.*
> *For a while, both are silent.*)

I'm really sorry. Will you...will you let me say I'm sorry?

LEAH. I was the one who let the knife slip.

DANIELLE. I didn't mean to upset you.

LEAH. It did just slip.

DANIELLE. And I'm sorry for what I said about Mirah. I
knew you saw each other for Shabbat sometimes, but, I
had no idea... And I'm sorry for saying I'd leave.

,

I'm still here, aren't I?

,

Are we okay?

> (*Pause.*)

LEAH. ...Are you finished?

DANIELLE. One minute.

,

There.

> (*The bandage wrapped,* **LEAH** *goes to the boxes.*)

LEAH. I've never seen these.

DANIELLE. Why would you have seen them?

LEAH. Usually Mirah and I just talk crap. Or go through
her books.

DANIELLE. That's what you've been doing when you bunk
off school?

LEAH. Sometimes the wifi works. We watch Netflix. Or Gogglebox.

DANIELLE. I cannot picture Aunt Mirah watching Gogglebox.

LEAH. She says it keeps her in touch with the youth. So she can relate to her students.

DANIELLE. I'd ask why you don't count as 'the youth', but...

LEAH. Look at this! It's your Batmitzvah invitation.

DANIELLE. Oh my god.

LEAH. What are those doodles round the sides?

DANIELLE. They're roses.

LEAH. I forgot you used to draw! It's actually not shit.

DANIELLE. I can't believe Aunt Mirah kept the invite.

LEAH. Did she even go to your Batmitzvah?

DANIELLE. "Did she go".

,

Don't you remember what happened?

LEAH. Um. Some uncles lifted you on a chair. I ate so many brownies I threw up on the rabbi's shoes.

,

I was eight years old.

DANIELLE. First of all, Mirah turned up late.

LEAH. The fashionable way.

DANIELLE. No. No, it was midway through the service. She was wearing the most 'look-at-me' outfit with these massive purple flowers on it, and like, a lace train thing. So obnoxious. Then at the party she and Mum had this huge argument.

LEAH. Seriously?

DANIELLE. Obviously it was Mirah who set it off.

LEAH. What did she do?

DANIELLE. She said something about Mum. "Being the smug Jewish Mother."

LEAH. Oh.

DANIELLE. Of course Mirah had no clue how much work Mum and I had put into the whole thing. And all my friends heard the two of them screaming during Hava Nagila. I remember thinking, it's my Batmitzvah. It was meant to be special. And Mirah and Mum ruined it, and…and I spent the rest of the day trying not to cry.

,

I didn't cry. Obviously. I pretended I didn't care.

,

That's why we didn't see Mirah for years. After that, Mum wouldn't talk to her.

(A beat.)

LEAH. She's good at that.

DANIELLE. Aunt Mirah?

LEAH. Mum. Not talking.

(Another beat.)

DANIELLE. Leah, you know Mum was worried about you today.

LEAH. …You spoke to her?

DANIELLE. You ran away.

LEAH. And she answered the phone?

DANIELLE. She called back this afternoon. She said she hadn't got my messages earlier because of the time difference.

LEAH. So she cares about me when I'm not around? Jokes.

DANIELLE. That's not it. You know it's not. She misses you.

,

You should talk to her.

LEAH. Don't have anything to say.

DANIELLE. You're so similar.

,

She says you don't reply to her texts. Why not?

> (**LEAH** *turns back to the boxes.*)

LEAH. Where are those reviews then?

DANIELLE. Leah.

> (**LEAH** *looks through boxes.*)

Did you hear what I said?

LEAH. You said you found Mirah's old reviews. I want to see.

DANIELLE. But...

(Giving in.) They're in this one.

> (*As they look through the reviews,* **MIRAH**
> *enters; one of Leah's memories.*)

They're all...they're all in pieces.

> (**MIRAH** *uses a pair of scissors to cut up a*
> *newspaper. When she speaks,* **DANIELLE**
> *can't hear.*)

MIRAH. I'm rather fucking flattered they reviewed me in print. Broadsheets like this don't grow on trees.

LEAH. 'A Convoluted Look At Judaism's Oldest Demons'.

MIRAH. I find it therapeutic to hack through the critique. Want to try?

LEAH. *(To* **DANIELLE.***)* Mirah cuts up her bad reviews. I'd forgotten.

DANIELLE. But then why does she keep them?

MIRAH. The things they're saying about me! Like they have any idea who I am. And the connotations – look at my photo. Always in profile. Why do you think that is?

DANIELLE. Seriously, she kept a one-star review. If anyone wrote this about me, I'd...

LEAH. Hunt them down?

DANIELLE. ...I was going to say hide. In a hole. And never show my face again.

*(***LEAH** *turns to address* **MIRAH.***)*

LEAH. Why don't you just not read them?

DANIELLE. Right. I wouldn't. I couldn't read them.

MIRAH. I'd rather know what people are saying about me. That way I can decide whether there's any truth in it. And whether to retaliate.

LEAH. Retaliate?

MIRAH. Only if it's necessary.

LEAH. *(To* **DANIELLE.***)* This book was about the mazzikim.

MIRAH. Translation: 'harmful spirit'. Invisible demons. Winged. Feet like a bird. "If the eye had the power to see them, no creature could endure the mazzikim."

DANIELLE. *(To* **LEAH.***)* Wait, isn't this one of the quotes on your wall?

MIRAH. The references are scattered throughout the Talmud, but they're illogical. Some interpret them as literal demons, others as a metaphor for fear, anger, hate.

LEAH. *(To* **DANIELLE.***)* What do you mean on my wall?

DANIELLE. I just mean...the notes you've been writing.

LEAH. Hang on.

> (*Our focus shifts from* **MIRAH**. **LEAH** *is now back in the present.*)

You read those?

DANIELLE. I had a look...

LEAH. I told you not to.

DANIELLE. I'm not sure you actually –

LEAH. Those are private.

DANIELLE. Really? Because they're kind of on display.

'

Sorry. Do you want to tell me what they mean?

LEAH. If you've read them, I don't need to.

DANIELLE. Are they based on Mirah's research?

LEAH. I wanted to find out what the noises are.

DANIELLE. Noises?

LEAH. I told you. I've been hearing things since I got here. It started yesterday, right after I found Mirah. While we waited for the ambulance.

DANIELLE. ...Were you panicking?

LEAH. I think I know why the noises started. It's because of... Don't laugh.

DANIELLE. Why would I laugh?

LEAH. I think it's 'cause of what the boy did. 'Cause he hurt Mirah.

DANIELLE. I don't follow.

LEAH. Mirah told me once that people make demons when they do bad things. I think what I've been hearing is something he left.

DANIELLE. ...Or. He's just a guy. Just an ordinary –

LEAH. I'm telling you, the cottage never used to be like this. It used to feel safe.

DANIELLE. The stuff Mirah writes about isn't real. You do know that? Are you sure that Mirah's, you know, a good influence?

LEAH. Is that what you think or what Dad thinks?

DANIELLE. I'm just saying, you taking off, running here. Your plan to frame this boy, for some kind of...revenge. It's a bit...

LEAH. A bit what?

DANIELLE. Unhinged.

LEAH. When that boy hurt Mirah, that was unhinged. That was... it was as good as attacking me. Us. And you don't know her like I do. You never will.

> (*A beat.* **DANIELLE** *moves to put away the boxes.*)

DANIELLE. Let me put these away.

LEAH. I'm not finished yet.

> (**LEAH** *grabs at the boxes, but one of them opens and the contents spill to the floor.* **DANIELLE** *tries to help.*)

I can do it.

> (*As both of them reach to pick up the mess, they freeze.*)

DANIELLE. Oh.

LEAH. It's a...

DANIELLE. It's an ultrasound.

LEAH. I know what it is.

DANIELLE. It's private. Put it back.

LEAH. It's dated twelve years ago. Mirah had just moved here.

(A pause.)

I don't understand.

DANIELLE. I mean, whoever it was with, they're not around.

LEAH. She didn't say anything.

DANIELLE. Why would she? You've only known her a few years, and this was twelve years ago. But Mirah and Mum were still speaking, so I'm sure we'd have known if...if it became more than this.

,

Look, if Mirah never told you, you should respect that.

LEAH. But. I always thought she came here to be by herself. "Lone woman in the woods."

DANIELLE. Maybe you don't know her as well as you thought.

(Time starts to shift.)

Scene Four

(Now – continuous / Four years ago.)

*(**MIRAH** addresses **LEAH** from the past. **DANIELLE** is still there, in the present.)*

MIRAH. Well. Make yourself at home.

*(**LEAH** can see **MIRAH**, but **DANIELLE** can't. **DANIELLE** picks up the scans.)*

DANIELLE. I'm going to put these away, okay?

*(**MIRAH** speaks to **LEAH**, entirely within the memory.)*

MIRAH. It looks like you're stuck with me.

LEAH. *(To **MIRAH**.)* I didn't realise... I didn't mean to dig this up.

*(**DANIELLE** leaves.)*

(The time clicks into place.)

Scene Five

(Four years ago. Mirah's cottage.)

*(For **MIRAH**, the scene simply continues. She tries to act welcoming to **LEAH** but is painfully awkward.)*

MIRAH. Would you like to sit down?

*(**LEAH** is now thirteen years old.)*

LEAH. Um. No.

MIRAH. *(Child-speak.)* Okey-doke. No problemo!

,

Last time I saw you, you were eight years old. You'd just eaten far too much dessert, and then you went up to the rabbi, and...never mind, I don't remember. But now, here you are. You're like a real person.

*(**LEAH** is unamused.)*

Do you want to see your room?

LEAH. I'm going home on Sunday.

MIRAH. ...Correct.

LEAH. So it's not my room. Just a place to sleep.

MIRAH. Well I'm grateful your Dad dumped you here. It gave me an excuse to change the sheets. And believe me, I only do laundry under threat or at gunpoint.

LEAH. What's the wifi?

MIRAH. Oh, I think it's down again today.

,

It might be down again.

LEAH. What?

MIRAH. That happens sometimes. Piece of crap really. At least today it's Shabbat, so maybe the router wanted her day of rest.

LEAH. Fuck.

> *(Glancing at **MIRAH**.)*

Sorry.

MIRAH. FUCK!

> *(**LEAH** stares.)*

Just joining in. Drink? Tea?

LEAH. I hate tea.

MIRAH. We have strong opinions! That's good. Let me think, I have...water...squash...six months out of date, but it probably won't kill you.

LEAH. Do you have Wotsits?

MIRAH. I doubt it. One moment.

> *(**MIRAH** sweeps off to look in the kitchen. **LEAH** glances around the room with curiosity.)*

(Offstage.) No... No... That tupperware's growing legs. Horrendous.

> *(She returns, proclaiming to the sky, perhaps putting on an accent.)*

My cupboard is bare. What kind of Jewish kitchen is this!

LEAH. You're weird.

MIRAH. What did you expect, lone woman in the woods? That's how your parents see me. Don't tell your Dad I said that.

LEAH. Dad said you were 'quirky'.

MIRAH. I see. That's code for totally off my noodle.

LEAH. Danielle called you a lunatic.

MIRAH. Well that's not code is it, that's just rude.

,

Did you believe them?

>   (**LEAH** *shrugs.*)

Well, now you're here you can make up your own mind.

LEAH. I think...I think you're as messy as I am.

,

Is that why we've not visited?

MIRAH. Let's say my sister and I – your Mum and I... Let's say we never really got on.

>   (*A beat.*)

LEAH. Have you talked to her?

MIRAH. Hmm?

LEAH. Nothing.

>   (**MIRAH** *realises she's brought up a potential bombshell.*)

MIRAH. No, I haven't. Not for years.

,

I had no idea she was planning to leave.

,

How are you doing?

LEAH. Who even cares?

>   (*A beat.* **MIRAH** *looks startled and slightly sad.*)

MIRAH. When your Dad called me on Tuesday, asking if I'd like to see you this weekend, I got so excited. Of course, I thought he was finally inviting me to your Batmitzvah.

I was already bracing myself for a long chat about the fish course with your Dad's parents. Cunts.

'

Then I realised that he was calling to grovel. And to check that if I agreed to have you stay, I wouldn't accidentally lose you in the woods. But you know, I've been really looking forward to you being here.

'

I'm sorry your Batmitzvah was cancelled.

LEAH. Mum didn't want it to happen.

MIRAH. I'm sure that isn't true.

LEAH. She didn't want a family.

MIRAH. What makes you say that?

LEAH. I heard her arguing.

MIRAH. Leah… This… Your Mum leaving… It isn't your fault. A Batmitzvah is meant to be a celebration. But it also means the whole family's watching. Everything on show. I might not have answers, but based on when she and I were younger I have theories.

LEAH. What was she like?

(*A beat.*)

MIRAH. When we were children, I would see how much she wanted be perfect. To be the good one. I was fine being the weirdo, but she took it all upon herself. And then, how to say this…being perfect just didn't fit.

LEAH. It's still Mum's fault.

MIRAH. People find it easy to blame the woman. We're easy targets. Especially if we're a bit different.

(**MIRAH** *takes a book from the shelf.*)

Here. A Batmitzvah present.

LEAH. Um...

MIRAH. It's about Lilith. Better reviews than my last book, but it didn't even pay for a new boiler.

(**LEAH** *takes the book with suspicion.*)

LEAH. Your book as a present? Danielle said you were cheap.

MIRAH. Haven't you heard of Lilith? The first woman?

LEAH. Thanks, but, nah.

(*She turns to her phone.* **MIRAH** *persists.*)

MIRAH. Lilith came before Eve. They don't teach it at *Cheder*, but she came from the same place as Adam: the dirt. Lilith didn't behave the way she was expected to. Same dirt, she thought, means the same. Equal. So, Lilith would not lie beneath Adam –

LEAH. "Lie beneath".

MIRAH. Sexually, yes.

(**LEAH** *smirks despite herself.*)

And she refused to do his bidding. And because she couldn't stand being told what to do, she left. She flew away... What do you think Adam did after Lilith left?

'

He complained. He begged to have his woman back. And so, God sent three of his angels to hunt her down and drown her. But she persuaded them to let her go. Instead, she was banished. Adam replaced her, and those who remembered made up stories.

LEAH. What did they say?

MIRAH. Over time, the stories transformed her into a frightening, uncontrollable creature who births succubi, flies by night, kills infants. *Lilith.* Translation: 'night monster'. Winged. Wild. A demon.

(A beat.)

LEAH. But those stories were made up?

MIRAH. Correct.

LEAH. But... That's not fair.

MIRAH. You've just summarised my book in three words.

(There's a rustling from the corner of the room.)

Oh! Someone's come to say hello. It's Babs. Barbara.
Meet Barbara.

,

She won't bite. Say hello Babs. You know, like Streisand?

(Singing from Funny Girl, *half to* **LEAH**, *half
to the cat.)*

"People, people who need people..." No?

LEAH. Has she got...?

MIRAH. What? Oh. Oh bollocks.

*(**MIRAH** leans down to the floor.)*

Oh dear, she's left us a present. Are you squeamish?

LEAH. Is it dead? Are those its guts? Cool.

MIRAH. No then, to being squeamish.

LEAH. Can I touch it?

MIRAH. No. You'll catch something.

LEAH. Like, salmonella?

MIRAH. Maybe if you eat it. Please don't eat it.

LEAH. The blood's all over its feathers.

*(**MIRAH** drops a pair of gloves beside **LEAH**.)*

MIRAH. You wanted to pick it up.

LEAH. Where are you going?

MIRAH. Garden.

LEAH. But, it's raining.

MIRAH. Barely a drizzle. Coming?

> (**LEAH** *gathers the dead bird. Outside, we hear the rain.*)

LEAH. Aren't you going to throw it in the bin?

MIRAH. That would be disrespectful. Now, if you don't mind grabbing the trowel, we can put it in the rock garden.

LEAH. What's a trowel?

MIRAH. It's... I'll get it.

> (**MIRAH** *brings the trowel over.*)

LEAH. Can I do the digging?

MIRAH. Oh. I don't like anyone else to... if you like.

> (**LEAH** *and* **MIRAH** *kneel down on the soil of the rock garden.*)

Try here.

LEAH. Just like...?

MIRAH. Yes. A little deeper.

> (*Under* **MIRAH**'s *direction,* **LEAH** *digs.*)

Now cover it up.

,

Good. Now, we mark it with stones.

> (*They take a stone and put it on the soil.*)

There we go.

LEAH. What do the stones do?

MIRAH. Lots of things. They make the memory permanent, even if...even if its death was far too soon.

LEAH. Is that what the other rocks are for? Dead birds?

MIRAH. Some of them are just markers.

LEAH. That one?

MIRAH. That one was a mouse.

LEAH. What was that over there, with the big stone?

> (**LEAH** *points to a spot at the edge of the rock garden.* **MIRAH** *is silent.*)

Was that a bird?

MIRAH. No... No.

> (*They sit looking at the stone.* **MIRAH** *is moved but tries to hide it. Finally she gets up.*)

Come on, or you'll catch a cold. Then what would your Dad say?

LEAH. Are you okay?

MIRAH. Why wouldn't I be?

> (**MIRAH** *leaves.*)

Scene Six

(*Now. Evening.* **DANIELLE** *brings in two bowls of pasta.*)

DANIELLE. The sauce options here are ketchup or marmite. Sorry, but that's the menu and you can't choose nothing.

,

Don't say you're not hungry. When was the last time you had a proper meal?

(**LEAH** *half-heartedly takes a bowl.* **DANIELLE** *hovers, restless.*)

It's getting dark.

,

Dad still doesn't know we're here. That I've even found you. Mum doesn't either.

,

Maybe, after we've eaten, we can drive out and call them –

LEAH. Pass the ketchup.

(**DANIELLE** *obliges, then takes a bite from her own bowl.*)

DANIELLE. This is awful.

LEAH. Yup.

(*They eat in silence.*)

Mirah always seemed like such a loner –

DANIELLE. Leah, can't we talk about something else?

LEAH. I don't think she has friends in the village. The nearest synagogue is ages away so she never goes.

DANIELLE. So what?

LEAH. I just thought she was always like that. But then. The ultrasound.

DANIELLE. You've only known Aunt Mirah three years.

LEAH. Four.

DANIELLE. That's nothing for an old person.

LEAH. I just thought she always wanted to be alone.

DANIELLE. I guess you can't assume.

LEAH. But it makes the name-calling in the village worse. Calling her a witch.

DANIELLE. I mean, at least she won't be living here much longer.

LEAH. What do you mean?

DANIELLE. She's trying to sell the cottage.

,

Dad told me last week. She called him out of the blue asking about mortgage brokers. But apparently this cottage is basically falling down, so, she's stuck.

,

I wondered if she hadn't told you.

LEAH. But. That isn't true.

DANIELLE. I mean what do I know about mortgages? But I guess with everything going on here in the village...

LEAH. Why did Dad tell you and not me? Why didn't Mirah tell me? She can't leave and not say anything.

DANIELLE. Don't be stupid. She'll tell you if she actually goes anywhere.

LEAH. But she can't just decide –

DANIELLE. You need to grow up.

(A faint scuttle.)

LEAH. Stop treating me like I'm thick.

DANIELLE. Then stop making a thing out of everything. Jesus. Talking to you's like – I can't say anything without...

,

Can we just eat dinner and go home?

LEAH. You can't handle being around me for more than ten minutes.

DANIELLE. We've been here a solid two and a half hours, actually.

LEAH. Mirah's the only one who can stand it.

DANIELLE. Now you're talking crap.

LEAH. Am I? Dad's always at work. You're never home.

DANIELLE. I'm literally living there.

LEAH. But you always leave.

(A beat.)

DANIELLE. When do I leave?

,

You're the one who ran away yesterday, so I don't know / what –

LEAH. After Mum left, you left straight away.

DANIELLE. That was years ago. And I went to uni.

LEAH. You could have waited.

DANIELLE. Postponed my degree?

LEAH. Yes.

,

You didn't visit. And now you're home you're never here. You weren't even around for *Yom Kippur*. You're only living with us to save money.

DANIELLE. Is that what you think?

LEAH. You got to get your perfect degree, your perfect job. John Lewis, for fuck's sake.

DANIELLE. It's not exactly perfect you / know –

LEAH. Can you be more of a suck-up?

DANIELLE. Do you want to know why I moved home? I moved home because Dad asked me to.

LEAH. Why would he / do that?

DANIELLE. Because of you, Leah.

(A beat. Another scuttle.)

LEAH. You were sent to spy on me?

DANIELLE. He's worried. He tries not to show it, but... you refuse to talk to him about anything. You won't even talk to Mum.

LEAH. Why should I? She's in another country.

DANIELLE. Because... Because she tries talking to you. She's trying to make it right.

LEAH. That's funny. No, it is. She's the one who left without telling anyone. Anyway, I'm over it.

(A feather floats down from the ceiling.)

DANIELLE. Have you thought that maybe you have no idea what it was like, at home, before she left?

LEAH. I was right there.

DANIELLE. Dad said you were too young, so... You didn't see everything.

LEAH. What do you mean?

DANIELLE.   She was unhappy, okay. Unhappy as in, miserable. And not 'cause of us, or Dad. It's just that for ages the doctors ignored her. And then the medication didn't work. But she's doing better. I think hearing it from her would help.

LEAH. Why?

DANIELLE. You're just...so angry all the time.

LEAH. Maybe I'm allowed to be angry. Maybe I'm fucking justified in being a bit angry. Maybe that doesn't make me broken, maybe it makes me –

DANIELLE. I didn't say broken, / I –

LEAH. Maybe it makes me normal. Have you thought about that?

,

And I know more than you think. About Mum. Life didn't stop 'cause you weren't there. Dad was trying to pretend everything was fine, but if she hadn't been planning my fucking Batmitzvah – if I hadn't been around at all – she'd have stayed. *That's* why I don't speak to her. I'm why she left.

(Beat.)

Do you have nothing to say?

DANIELLE. Do you seriously think that?

LEAH. You act like you know everything, but you don't. You pretend things are okay when they're not. You never get angry.

DANIELLE. I do too.

LEAH. You never get proper angry. Or show any real emotion. That's weirder. Actually. You're just empty.

(There is a noise from inside the cottage, like a creak or a groan. **DANIELLE** *looks around, startled, upset.)*

Go on, tell me I'm wrong.

(Another noise.)

Nothing. You're just a heartless nothing.

DANIELLE. What is that?

LEAH. You can hear that now?

DANIELLE. What is it?

LEAH. I told you.

DANIELLE. But... There must be something in the pipes.

LEAH. My sister the plumber.

DANIELLE. You're making jokes now? After saying what you just...

,

Are you doing this?

LEAH. How?

,

I told you I've been trying to work it out. You read the quote about the *mazzikim*. Harmful spirits. Demons.

DANIELLE.   Leah...Mirah writes about stuff. It doesn't mean she believes it. Demons aren't even Jewish.

LEAH. Aren't you listening?

DANIELLE. They're not part of normal Judaism.

LEAH. Think about the radio. It doesn't work anymore.

DANIELLE. Nothing in this place works.

LEAH. It switched on by itself.

DANIELLE. Wiring issues...

LEAH. That window keeps shaking.

DANIELLE. Have you heard of the wind?

LEAH. I keep seeing feathers.

DANIELLE. Feathers?

LEAH. Floating down. Out the corner of my eye.

DANIELLE. ...Does the cat ever bring in birds?

,

There you go.

LEAH. No, that's not it.

DANIELLE. But do you hear yourself? It's insane to / think –

LEAH. Listen to me!

,

There's a quote in the Talmud, about how to tell if the *mazzikim* are really here.

(**LEAH** *finds one of the notes from her wall.*)

"If one wants to discover them, let him take sifted ashes and sprinkle around his bed, and in the morning he will see something like the footprints of a rooster."

,

I'm going to try it, tonight. Then at least we'll know if that's the type of demon we're dealing with.

DANIELLE. The thing is. We are not staying the night.

LEAH. And there's an exorcism ritual we could try, from the sixteenth century. The sign that it's worked is if a candle goes out.

DANIELLE. Jesus.

LEAH. We'd have to be careful though, otherwise it could choke us.

DANIELLE. We are leaving. Right now.

(There's another noise, but this time it's from outside. It sounds like a snapping branch.)

(All noise inside the cottage stops. The sisters freeze.)

What was that?

(Another branch snaps.)

Did that come from outside?

(Silence.)

Where's the cat?

LEAH. Upstairs.

DANIELLE. Does anyone ever come here? Like, delivery people, or...

LEAH. Not at night.

*(**LEAH** moves towards the door.)*

DANIELLE. Leah, don't.

*(**LEAH** goes to the window.)*

LEAH. It's him. He got the message.

DANIELLE. Who?

LEAH. The boy.

,

Did you think I was making him up?

DANIELLE. ...Kind of?

,

What if he tries to come in... What if he –

(A car alarm goes off, harsh and loud, metres away from the house.)

Oh god oh god oh god.

LEAH. Shhh.

DANIELLE. But –

LEAH. I won't let him in. Promise.

> *(They wait.* **LEAH** *watches through the window. Finally:)*

He's gone.

DANIELLE. Don't –

> *(***LEAH** *runs outside. Reluctantly,* **DANIELLE** *follows. They stare across the garden, towards the driveway.)*

Has he slashed up my tires???

LEAH. Mirah's as well.

DANIELLE. How will we get home? If we call AA do you think they'll come tonight? Or maybe – maybe we could call Dad and, and –

LEAH. If you want to find somewhere with signal.

DANIELLE. Crap. Oh freaking crapping hell!

LEAH. That's more swearing than I've heard you swear ever.

DANIELLE. What do we do? Do you think he'll come back? Do you think he'll... I don't even understand why he'd... What's that?

> *(***LEAH** *has picked up a piece of paper from the ground.* **DANIELLE** *snatches it.)*

LEAH. He got my note.

DANIELLE. But I don't...

,

That's the message you sent him? The one where you told him you wanted to talk? You left this all over the village?

LEAH. They won't understand.

DANIELLE. They're not village idiots!

LEAH. That message was for him, after what he said before. I did just want to talk.

DANIELLE. *(Reading the note aloud.)* "You angered the witch. Meet me alone."

,

Get inside.

LEAH. But –

DANIELLE. Now.

> *(They return to the cottage.)*

LEAH. Are you locking him out or me in?

DANIELLE. This is because of you, and your stupid plan, and your stupid notes. I am so sick of your hormonal teenage drama.

> *(**DANIELLE** rips up the note and throws it in the bin.)*

LEAH. I knew I shouldn't have told you.

DANIELLE. I'm going to call Dad, / and he –

LEAH. You never give a shit what I think.

DANIELLE. And he is going to call a taxi to come get us.

LEAH. I wish you'd never followed me here and I wish you'd stay the fuck away from me.

> *(A beat.)*

DANIELLE. I'm going to fix the landline.

> *(**DANIELLE** leaves, going into the next room. A feather falls from the ceiling, and **LEAH** watches it float down.)*

LEAH. You'll never fix the phone.

> *(She picks up the note.)*

"You angered the witch. Meet me alone." "Meet me alone..."

> *(She looks up. Perhaps she addresses the audience. Perhaps she speaks to herself.)*

He didn't bring a car. That means he walked here along the river, through the woods.

'

Through the woods.

> *(The broken window creaks open.)*

> *(With new resolve, **LEAH** climbs through the window and out of the cottage.)*

ACT III

Scene One

*(Now. Night. **DANIELLE** enters and finds the room empty. She sees the open window.)*

*(She steps out into the front garden, wondering whether to go after **LEAH**. It starts to rain.)*

(Helplessly, she goes back inside.)

(She starts to tidy. A feather falls but she doesn't see.)

(Against her better judgement, she turns to the books.)

DANIELLE. "If the eye had the power to see them, no creature could endure the *mazzikim*. They are more numerous than we are and they surround us like a ridge around a field. Every one among us has a thousand on his left hand and ten thousand on his right hand."

(The night grows darker.)

"Fatigue in the knees comes from them. The wearing out of the clothes of the scholars is due to their rubbing against them. The bruising of the feet comes from them. If one wants to discover them, let him take sifted ashes and sprinkle around his bed, and in the morning he will see something like the footprints of a rooster."

*(Behind **DANIELLE**, a shadowed figure – the figure of a winged woman – begins to appear in the window.)*

(There is a crack of thunder and lightning floods the room. It lights the face of the woman.)

*(**DANIELLE** spins round, but the face is gone.)*

*(A scuttling begins, a creeping sound which seems to come from different parts of the cottage. **DANIELLE** looks around her, scared, struggling to make sense of the noises.)*

Scene Two

(Now. The woods. Night.)

*(**LEAH** weaves her way along the footpath.)*

*(Through the trees, we can just make out **MIRAH**, or at least a version of **MIRAH**. Not present-day **MIRAH**. Not past **MIRAH**. Imaginary **MIRAH**? Maybe.)*

MIRAH. Because Lilith couldn't stand being told what to do, she left. She flew away.

LEAH. Because I can't stand being told what to do, I left.

MIRAH. She took flight into the wilderness.

LEAH. I ran away to the woods. Mirah's woods. And I realise it's fucking freezing.

MIRAH. The night grew darker.

LEAH. I don't have my coat with me, and it starts to rain.

,

For the first time since leaving home, I hear my Dad's voice, saying, "You should learn to do what you're told. Come home. Do what your sister tells you."

MIRAH. But she was never very good at following orders.

LEAH. I know this path.

MIRAH. She knows this path.

LEAH. When I'm here, no one can reach me.

MIRAH. She thinks she's invincible.

LEAH. It's so dark that the banks of mud become pits. I feel like I'm being pulled into the ground.

MIRAH. In the darkness, she moves by muscle memory.

LEAH. How's the boy been doing it? I know this place, but he doesn't.

MIRAH. Follow the river's whisper.

LEAH. He's only been here one, two, three times before. To bully us. This was meant to be where I was safe. But now... he can't have gone far.

MIRAH. Here there are roots, knotted –

LEAH. Grabbing at me.

MIRAH. Branches crouching –

LEAH. Stroking my face.

MIRAH. The rain gets worse.

LEAH. The rain gets worse.

MIRAH. The ground gets wet.

LEAH. The ground is wet, and the trees are thick around me –

LEAH & MIRAH. Listening.

LEAH. Then I see the river.

MIRAH. What do you want?

LEAH. I want...I want to find him. For him to confess. To say sorry.

MIRAH. And if he doesn't?

(Beat.)

LEAH. I wish I'd had more to eat earlier. More sleep. And just when I feel like I'm hallucinating...

(We see the boy's figure in shadow.)

There he is. I see him.

(She stands, frozen.)

He's here. My plan worked. And…and he's real. He's just a boy. A teenager, like me. He's real… He's…scared?

,

I realise, this boy has no power.

MIRAH. You've made a mistake.

LEAH. I've made a mistake. He has no power. Not alone.

,

I reach for my phone in my pocket, so I can record what he says. But, I feel something soft.

> *(Out of her pocket, **LEAH** takes out a feather. She looks at it, confused.)*

MIRAH. You've made a mistake.

LEAH. I realise, too late, that he can't see what it is in the dark. 'Cause next he reaches into his pocket. And I see the faintest glint. He has a knife.

,

He has a knife!

> *(Beat.)*

MIRAH. Run.

LEAH. I try to run.

MIRAH. But she trips.

LEAH. We fall.

MIRAH. The two of them fall – into the river.

LEAH. I…

MIRAH. The water's shallow.

LEAH. I can't…

MIRAH. It's fucking freezing.

LEAH. I...

MIRAH. It's too late to talk.

(There is a crack of thunder.)

Scene Three

(Now. Night. The rain has become a storm.
DANIELLE *waits inside Mirah's cottage,*
shaken and jittery. She's a mess. Her ankles
are covered in mud.)

(Unseen by **DANIELLE**, **LEAH** *approaches the*
front door from outside. She's shivering. Her
clothes are soaked.)

(When **LEAH** *enters,* **DANIELLE** *jumps, grabs*
the large kitchen knife, and points it towards
LEAH.*)*

DANIELLE. Jesus fuck Christ on a bike!

'

Leah! Leah thank god.

(For perhaps the first time in years, **DANIELLE**
hugs **LEAH**. *Meanwhile* **LEAH** *is shell-shocked*
from earlier. It's very awkward.)

LEAH. What happened to you?

DANIELLE. To me? What about you? You're…you're soaking
wet.

LEAH. *(Trying to keep it together.)* I fell. In the river.

DANIELLE. Oh my God, are you okay?

LEAH. Could you get me a towel?

DANIELLE. I was scared I'd lost you.

LEAH. …I'm here.

DANIELLE. I didn't know where you'd gone.

LEAH. Woods.

DANIELLE. Do you want a tea? A bath? Shall I check if the
boiler's working?

LEAH. Hate tea.

DANIELLE. I tried to go out and look for you.

LEAH. Is that why you look a mess?

> *(Overwhelmed,* **DANIELLE** *crumples onto a chair, fighting back tears.)*

Oh come on. I take it back. You look awesome.

DANIELLE. No. I do look a mess.

> *(***DANIELLE*** *tries to pull herself together, but can't.)*

I just. I didn't know which way you'd gone, or if you'd got yourself hurt. And I swear I really tried, I tried to follow you.

LEAH. That's why your hair –

DANIELLE. Like a bird's nest. And my make-up. It was so dark, and I don't know the woods, and...and I stepped in a puddle!

LEAH. Not a puddle.

DANIELLE. But that's not. That's not why I... While I was waiting here, I thought I heard...

,

I thought I'd pushed you away. And then if something happened to you, it would be my fault.

LEAH. Hey, who says you get all the credit?

> *(***DANIELLE*** *lets out a laugh that becomes a sob.)*

Do *you* want a tea?

DANIELLE. No. Yes. You've never offered to get me anything like that in your life.

LEAH. Shit.

,

Okay.

(**LEAH** *starts to head towards the kitchen.*)

DANIELLE. No, wait.

,

Don't leave me alone.

(*A beat.* **LEAH** *fights to hold it together.*)

LEAH. What happened while I was gone?

,

I'd really like a towel.

(**DANIELLE** *looks around the room and finds one of Mirah's shawls.*)

DANIELLE. Here. Stay.

(*She drapes it around* **LEAH**.)

I'm sorry for what I said. "Hormonal teenage drama." I didn't mean it.

LEAH. Well. I didn't mean what I said either.

DANIELLE. I don't even remember.

LEAH. You're not empty.

DANIELLE. Oh. It's fine.

LEAH. It's not. I hate myself.

DANIELLE. Don't. Seriously. Besides... You're right.

LEAH. ...Wow.

DANIELLE. It's like I've tried for so long to be okay with everything, and to push it all away. Anything that feels a bit weird, or scary. But now when I actually try to feel something real, I just. Feel nothing.

LEAH. But you're always so perfect. Everything you do.

DANIELLE. I hate it.

LEAH. Everyone loves you.

DANIELLE. People 'like' me. No one...no one 'feels' much about me. Everyone feels strongly about you.

LEAH. Yeah. 'Cause you're the suck-up, I'm the fuck up.

DANIELLE. No, but. You get to be angry. You get to be difficult. I never let myself do that. I thought when I went to uni maybe I'd be able to let go, but.

,

I guess I thought, if I stayed away from our family, I could somehow be me. But I think me is just a bit...a bit disappointing.

LEAH. I feel strongly about you. You're the most annoying person I know.

      (**DANIELLE** *laughs.*)

DANIELLE. You know I didn't stay away because of you? Neither did Mum. You didn't make her leave.

LEAH. I just wanted to make it right.

      (*A feather floats across the room as* **LEAH** *shivers. A faint scuttling begins, so soft we can almost believe* **DANIELLE** *can't hear it.*)

DANIELLE. What happened out there?

LEAH. I told you. I fell in the river.

DANIELLE. Okay, well, we're going to have to stay the night here. But that's okay, because I'll call in sick tomorrow. And that's fine, because all my colleagues are knobs.

LEAH. Really?

DANIELLE. All of them.

LEAH. Even John?

DANIELLE. Who's –

LEAH. John...Lewis.

DANIELLE. That's so crap.

LEAH. My game's off today.

(**DANIELLE** *laughs and moves closer to* **LEAH**.)

DANIELLE. Do you know the real reason why I wasn't around for *Yom Kippur*? They'd scheduled this big meeting at work. I didn't know how to ask for the time off.

LEAH. But, why not?

DANIELLE. I was...embarrassed? They're making a song and dance right now, about being inclusive. But then you look at the people at the top and think, they're all the same. And I'm lucky. I can look the same as them. But then there's a comment, or an assumption, and I remember. I remember how people like us get demonised. And the blood libel started in England, didn't it. The blood libel. Accusing Jews of drinking the blood of children, which sounds fucking ridiculous until you realise that those lies keep coming back. So, yes, I could have asked for the day off at work. But sometimes it feels easier to just blend in.

,

I don't know. You think you're invisible, until you're not.

(*A beat.*)

LEAH. I didn't know you felt like that.

DANIELLE. Well, I'm good at hiding it.

,

That's the worst thing about what happened here, with Mirah. She's never tried to hide who she is. But then that boy wrote that thing in the dirt... I'm sorry I pretended it was nothing. It wasn't. It's terrifying.

(The scuttling grows ever so slightly louder.)

LEAH. I need to tell you something.

,

I found the boy.

(DANIELLE stares at LEAH.)

DANIELLE. You found him?

LEAH. Yes?

DANIELLE. Did he try to hurt you? Are you okay?

LEAH. No. Yes. No. He had a knife.

DANIELLE. A knife!

LEAH. But he didn't...he didn't use it. I tried to run away –

DANIELLE. Jesus –

LEAH. But then I slipped. Him too. We both fell in the river.

DANIELLE. Oh my god.

LEAH. It was fucking awful. And fucking freezing. But I got out. And I saw him do the same. I think he was in shock. Like me.

DANIELLE. Nothing like you.

LEAH. And then...he ran away.

DANIELLE. Ran away?

LEAH. I think he might have been scared.

DANIELLE. So, he's gone?

LEAH. I think so?

(The scuttling gets subtly louder.)

I spent this whole time thinking that if I could just get him to admit what he did, it would make it okay. I thought I was on this mission.

,

And then I thought he was the reason for the noises. That he created these demons 'cause of what he did...

,

But really, he's just a sad, stupid kid. Maybe showing off to his friends. Maybe a total loner and just not quite with it, you know? But isn't that...

DANIELLE. Mundane.

LEAH. Scary. I think it's scary. That someone so ordinary can think these things, and hurt Mirah. And...and get away with it. He didn't even say sorry!

DANIELLE. Leah, I don't know if he would have ever said that.

LEAH. But even after all this –

DANIELLE. But what could you have done? You couldn't hurt him back.

LEAH. But then what was this whole thing for?

DANIELLE. I...I don't know.

LEAH. So what was I doing? What was I thinking?

> (*There is a creak inside the cottage. Both* **LEAH** *and* **DANIELLE** *react.*)

And if the noises I've been hearing weren't because of him... Either I'm going mad –

DANIELLE. You're not.

LEAH. Or it's me. I made the demons.

DANIELLE. What are you talking about?

> (**MIRAH** *enters, speaking from a different space and time.*)

MIRAH. There's a tradition which says demons can be created by our deeds. It works both ways; when we do something good, it creates an angel. When we do something bad it creates... well, there you go.

LEAH. What's wrong with me?

DANIELLE. Don't say that.

LEAH. School's been worried. Dad's been worried. You even said Mum was worried 'cause I ran away.

DANIELLE. They just care about you.

LEAH. And look how I repay them. I even... I cut my fucking hand open. That isn't me.

> (*A loud creak from inside the house.* **LEAH** *shouts at the walls.*)

Shut up! Why won't you shut up?

DANIELLE. Leah.

LEAH. Did you hear that? Please tell me. Did you hear that?

DANIELLE. I heard it.

,

You are not mad, do you hear me? I've noticed the noises too.

LEAH. You have?

DANIELLE. I didn't want to hear them. But then, when I was here alone...

LEAH. So, the noises aren't in my head?

DANIELLE. No.

LEAH. But. The demons are meant to be personal. So, why can you hear them?

> (*Neither knows the answer.*)

DANIELLE. How do we get rid of them?

> (**LEAH** *turns to the house.*)

LEAH. Go on! Tell us. What are you?

DANIELLE. Can we not talk to them?

LEAH. I think I know what to do. You're going to hate it.

DANIELLE. Hate what?

LEAH. Sixteenth century exorcisms.

MIRAH. Step one: Question the demon.

LEAH. Step one: Question the demons.

> (**LEAH** *looks around her and addresses the shadows.*)

Why are you here?

(*To* **DANIELLE**.) I'm asking them why they're here.

DANIELLE. Jesus. Are you sure that's what we need to do?

LEAH. Danielle, do you trust me?

'

Do you trust me?

DANIELLE. Yes... Okay. You're in charge. Tell me what to do.

MIRAH. Recite incantations. Say a psalm.

LEAH. We recite a psalm, to cast away evil.

DANIELLE. I haven't read Hebrew since my Batmitzvah.

LEAH. Well I didn't even get a Batmizvah.

> (**MIRAH** *begins reciting the psalm in Hebrew.*)

MIRAH. ;יֹשֵׁב, בְּסֵתֶר עֶלְיוֹן
(*yo·shev be·se·ter el·yo·n.*)

> (**LEAH** *listens, and repeats, stiltedly.*)

LEAH. Yoshev...beseter...elyon.

DANIELLE. Wait, how do you know that?

*(**MIRAH** continues reciting the psalm as **LEAH** repeats it. The scuttling grows gradually louder. If there are any mirrors on set, **MIRAH** covers them with the shawl.)*

MIRAH. בְּצֵל שַׁדַּי, יִתְלוֹנָן

(be·tzel shadai yit·lo·nan.)

LEAH. Betzel shadai yitlonan.

DANIELLE. What's going on?

MIRAH. אֹמַר—לַיהוָה, מַחְסִי וּמְצוּדָתִי;   אֱלֹהַי, אֶבְטַח-בּוֹ

(o·mar la·shem mach·si u·me·tzu·da·ti; e·lo·hai ev·tach-bo.)

LEAH. Omar lashem machsi umetzudati; elohai evtach-bo.

*(To **DANIELLE**.)* Psalm ninety-one.

DANIELLE. ...

LEAH. Step two... What was step number two?

(She goes to her notes on the wall.)

Step two: Fumigation.

DANIELLE. Fumigation!

LEAH. Candles.

*(**LEAH** finds candles and begins lighting them.)*

Come on, help me.

*(**DANIELLE** obeys, joining **LEAH** as they light candles and place them around the room.)*

DANIELLE. Okay, now what?

LEAH. The next step is to demand that the demons go away.

DANIELLE. Right...

LEAH. *(To the room.)* Go away.

DANIELLE. That's it?

LEAH. *(To* **DANIELLE.***)* Shh.

(To the room, shouting.) Go away.

(For just a moment, everything is silent.)

(Then, a hundred shadows cross the wall. **DANIELLE** *lets out a small scream. Books fall.)*

(The shadows begin flitting like a thousand birds flying about the room.)

MIRAH. I must warn you, this demand comes with great danger.

LEAH. This is the most dangerous part.

MIRAH. If you're not careful, the demon will leave through an organ.

LEAH. If we're not careful, the demon will leave / through...

MIRAH. Sometimes, the throat. If you're not careful, it will choke you.

*(***LEAH** *grows tense.)*

LEAH. If they can leave through an organ...whose organ?

MIRAH. Traditionally, the way to tell if an exorcism has worked is if a candle blows out. And if it hasn't blown out, the traditional way to make the demon leave is to force it out through the toe.

*(***LEAH** *turns to* **DANIELLE.***)*

LEAH. You need to get out of here.

DANIELLE. What?

LEAH. What I said. You need to go.

,

You said I was in charge.

DANIELLE. But you just said this was dangerous.

LEAH. It's the next step.

DANIELLE. What is?

LEAH. I need to do this alone.

DANIELLE. But –

LEAH. You said you trusted me.

> (**LEAH** *leads* **DANIELLE** *to the door. She hugs* **DANIELLE. DANIELLE** *is confused.*)

I have to make it right.

> (**LEAH** *pushes* **DANIELLE** *out of the cottage and locks the door behind her. She turns back to* **MIRAH**.)

So now we make them leave. We demand that they leave. We...

> (*But* **MIRAH** *has vanished.* **LEAH** *looks around her, but* **MIRAH** *is nowhere to be seen.*)

Mirah?

> (*The shadows continue to move. The noises grow louder.*)

Mirah?

> (*Alone,* **LEAH** *breathes faster, beginning to panic.*)
>
> (*She grips the furniture, trying to control her breathing.*)

...In through the nose. Out through the mouth... In through the nose. Out through the mouth.

> (*Finally, she calms herself. She looks around. The candles haven't gone out. She returns to her notes.*)

If the candles haven't gone out...

>   (*Rummaging through the notes.*)

If the candles haven't gone out...

>   (*Finding the note.*)

You have to make it leave through the big toe.

,

Okay.

>   (**LEAH** *finds the kitchen knife as the noises grow in volume, pulsating to a rhythm until they sound like giant wings flapping.*)
>
>   (*She grasps the knife and raises it.*)
>
>   (*Then the broken window flies open, and* **DANIELLE** *climbs back inside the cottage.*)

DANIELLE. Leah!

LEAH. I told you to leave.

DANIELLE. Whatever you're doing, don't. Please.

LEAH. I have to finish the exorcism. I have to get them out.

DANIELLE. Don't you fucking dare!

LEAH. There's no other way.

>   (*For a moment the sisters stare at each other, their gazes locked. Then, on impulse,* **DANIELLE** *knocks over the candles and books, trying to break the ritual. But the candles are still lit; Mirah's shawl catches fire.*)
>
>   (*Not to be outdone,* **LEAH** *plunges the knife into her own toe and screams.*)
>
>   (*The fire catches and flames grow, lighting the room. The shadows rise too, taking on a life of their own.*)

Scene Four

(Later. First we hear voices. Murmuring.)

(Days pass. There are more voices. There are beeps.)

(Lights up on a hospital café. It's clinical; a little too bright.)

(MIRAH enters. For the first time, we see her in the present. She looks tired, more worn-down. She walks on crutches.)

(LEAH arrives. Her foot is in a bandage, but she's here as a visitor.)

LEAH. Snap.

MIRAH. *(Glancing at LEAH's injured foot.)* Oh. Now you're just a copycat.

,

How is Danielle?

LEAH. ...Better. The doctors say there'll be minimal scarring.

MIRAH. That's positive.

LEAH. Is it?

MIRAH. In the circumstances, yes.

,

You should stop blaming yourself.

LEAH. But she was helping me get out. She was helping me, and now... She was only at the cottage 'cause of me.

MIRAH. It was her choice.

LEAH. Because of me! Because I refused to go home when she wanted.

MIRAH. How does she feel about it?

LEAH. That's the worst part. She's being nice? She's got bandages all over her. She should hate me. But instead...

MIRAH. Maybe you should respect her opinion. For once.

,

How are you?

LEAH. Who even cares?

MIRAH. I do. Always.

> *(A small pause.)*

LEAH. The police want to see me again. About how the fire started.

MIRAH. I've told them the candle was an accident.

LEAH. I know.

MIRAH. I've told them –

LEAH. I know.

MIRAH. I'll make sure the insurance covers it. So really you did me a favour burning the place down.

,

Don't tell your Dad I said that.

LEAH. You never told me you wanted to move.

MIRAH. It's only a recent feeling. I wasn't sure how you'd take it. But there's been a shift recently, in the village. At least that's how it feels. Maybe it's just me getting old. But even if the feeling's only in my head, I have to trust it. I'm sorry. I should have told you.

> *(They both fall silent. Then* **LEAH** *leans closer, lowering her voice.)*

LEAH. We were doing an exorcism.

(**MIRAH** *looks at* **LEAH** *in surprise.*)

MIRAH. What?

LEAH. At the cottage. Like you told me.

MIRAH. For what?

LEAH. For the demons.

,

I thought at first that boy made them, when he hurt you. Then I realised, it was me all along.

,

The exorcism didn't work. But I keep having nightmares, on a loop. Because the candle didn't go out. It did the opposite. And I couldn't control them... I couldn't control the demons.

(**MIRAH** *looks uncomfortable; guilty.*)

MIRAH. These things aren't always literal, you know.

(**LEAH** *looks at* **MIRAH**, *crushed.*)

LEAH. What do you mean?

MIRAH. I don't know what you saw. I wasn't there. But we've spoken about a lot of things. I write a lot of things. But that's different to believing in them. Maybe I should have made that clearer.

LEAH. Oh...

(*Something vital between them has broken.* **MIRAH** *is keenly aware of this.*)

MIRAH. You'll still visit me, even if I'm living somewhere boring? You could still come round for Shabbat, or just pasta?

LEAH. Not pasta.

MIRAH. Pizza then.

LEAH. I'm not around next week. I'm spending some time with Mum.

> (**MIRAH** *tries to hide how much this hurts.*)

MIRAH. I didn't realise she was flying over.

LEAH. Danielle says it's time I got to know her again. She's my real Mum after all.

'

So. I'll see you around.

> (**LEAH** *starts to limp away.* **MIRAH** *is devastated.*)
>
> (*Just before* **LEAH** *leaves,* **MIRAH** *calls her back.*)

MIRAH. There is one thing I've been wondering. About the cottage.

LEAH. What?

MIRAH. It's something I was told after they went inside to inspect it. They asked if there were often birds around. And I said, yes, of course, it's by the woods. But then they said no, they meant inside.

'

What they said was, when they arrived to inspect the cottage, all the rooms were covered in ash. And apparently, all across the floor, there were footprints. Birds' footprints.

> (**LEAH** *goes back to* **MIRAH**, *enthralled. Faintly, we hear a scuttling. A final feather falls.*)

End

Milton Keynes UK
Ingram Content Group UK Ltd.
UKHW020807210923
429104UK00014B/346